Congress of American Knife Fighters

# KNIFE FIGHTING ENCYCLOPEDIA

## Volume 1: The Foundation

By W. Hock Hochheim

Lauric Press
P.O. Box 5372
Ft. Oglethorpe, GA 30742
**(706)** 866-2656

www.HocksCQC.com

The Knife Fighting Encyclopedia
By W. Hock Hochheim

**Additional titles by W. Hock Hochheim**

*Military Knife Combat*
*The Great Escapes of Pancho Villa*
*Shooting from the Hip*
*Find Missing Persons*
*Punches*

Copyright 1997 (First Edition)
Copyright 2000 (Second Edition)

ISBN 0-9657302

Published by Lauric Press
P.O. Box 5372
Fort Oglethorpe, GA 30742
(706) 866-2656

Congress of American Knife Fighters
Knife Fighters Encyclopedia

# Table of Contents

Introduction: The Knife: Its Mystique, Myths, Life,
Death and Knife Fighter Training ............................................ i

Answers From the President, W. Hock Hochheim ..................... viii

Chapter 1: Knife Fighting Encounters ......................................... 1
Encounter 1: Knife vs. Knife ..................................................... 1
Encounter 2: Knife vs. the Unarmed ......................................... 3
Encounter 3: You Are Unarmed, and the Enemy
Has a Knife ........................................................................ 3

Chapter 2: Basic Knife Fighting Strategies .................................. 5
Strategy 1: Overcoming the Fear of Knife Fighting ................. 5
Strategy 2: The Element of Surprise, Shock, and
Fight or Flight .................................................................... 10
Strategy 3: Armed vs. Armed Progression Strategy ............... 12
Strategy 4: Armed vs. Unarmed Progression Strategy .......... 13
Strategy 5: Unarmed and Fighting the Knife
Progression Strategy ......................................................... 14
Strategy 6: The Mad Rush ...................................................... 15
Strategy 7: The Law and You, After the Encounter ............... 16
Summary ................................................................................ 20

Chapter 3: Knife Selection ......................................................... 21
Selection 1: The Training Knife ............................................. 21
Selection 2: The Fighting Knife ............................................. 23

Chapter 4: Knife Fighting Grips ........................................................... 29
  Grip 1: The Saber Grip ................................................................. 29
  Grip 2: The Reverse, Concealed or "Icepick" Grip ....................... 33
  Grip 3: Switching Grips and Hands Drills ................................... 36
  Grip 4: Practice Drills ................................................................. 39
  Summary ...................................................................................... 41

Chapter 5: Knife-Carrying and Drawing ............................................. 43
  Consideration 1: Carry Sites on the Body ................................... 43
  Consideration 2: Drawing the Blade ........................................... 46

Chapter 6: Knife Fighting Stances and Strategies .............................. 51
  Strategy 1: Four Fundamental Knife Fighting Stances ................. 51
  Strategy 2: Two Strong-Sided Forward Basic Fighting Stances ... 55
  Strategy 3: The Window of Combat ............................................. 55
  Strategy 4: Which Hand Holds the Knife .................................... 58

Chapter 7: Knife Fighting Footwork ................................................... 59
  Strategy 1: Basic Footwork ......................................................... 59
  Strategy 2: Footwork Drills ......................................................... 61

Chapter 8: Knife Target Strategies ..................................................... 65
  Target Strategy 1: The Impact of Wounds on the Sane and Insane ... 65
  Target Strategy 2: Delay Wounds ............................................... 66
  Target Strategy 3: Immobilization Wounds ................................. 68
  Target Strategy 4: Killshots ........................................................ 68
  Target Strategy 5: Exiting Techniques ........................................ 70

Chapter 9: Saber Grip Knife Fighting Techniques .............................. 73
  Introduction ................................................................................ 73
  Exercise Set 1: Saber Quickfire Targeting ................................... 75
  Exercise Set 2: Saber Grip Hacking ............................................ 79
  Exercise Set 3: Saber Grip Slashing ........................................... 83
  Drill 1: Eight Angles of Saber Grip Slashing Knife Attack ......... 84
  Drill 2: Eight Angles of Saber Grip Multiple Slashing Knife Attack ... 87
  Drill 3: Eight Angles of Saber Slashing and Stab Attack ........... 92
  Drill 4: Ten Angles of Saber Grip Stabbing Knife Attack ........... 97
  Drill 5: Ten Angles Saber Grip Stabbing, and Slashing Knife Attack ... 100

Drill 6: Eight Angles of Saber Grip Hacking Drill ................................... 102
Drill 7: Presas Family 12 Angles of Attack ....................................... 105

Chapter 10: Reverse Grip Knife Fighting Techniques ......................... 111
Introduction ............................................................................... 111
Basic Exercises Set 1 ................................................................. 112
Basic Exercises Set 2 ................................................................. 116
Basic Exercises Set 3 ................................................................. 118
Drill 1: Eight Angles Reverse Grip Slashing Knife Attack ................. 121
Drill 2: Eight Angles Reverse Grip Slashing and Stabbing Knife Attack ......... 126
Drill 3: Reverse Grip Concealed Slash and Stab Combat Drill ............ 131

Chapter 11: Knife Blocking ............................................................ 139
Blocking Strategy 1: Pros and Cons ............................................. 139
Blocking Strategy 2: The Difference Between Aggression and Defensive Blocks ... 141
Drill 1: Six Angles, Saber Grip, Basic Knife Blocking Drill ............... 143
Drill 2: Six Angles, Reverse Grip, Basic Knife Blocking Drill ........... 145
Drill 3: Arm Stop/Block Drills ..................................................... 147
Drill 4: Presas 12 Angle Blocking Combat Drills ........................... 150
Drill 5: Advanced Counter Attack Follow Ups ............................... 157

Chapter 12: Knife Disarming ......................................................... 159
The Basic Disarms ..................................................................... 159
Verbal Disarms .......................................................................... 160
"Defang the Snake" Impact Disarms ............................................. 162
Wristlock/X-Pattern Style Disarms ............................................... 169
The Chaos Wrist-Ripper Disarm Drill ........................................... 173
The Wristlock Disarm Progression Drill ........................................ 175
The Push/Pull Disarm Progression ............................................... 184
The Reverse Grip, Push/Pull Series .............................................. 190
Summary ................................................................................... 192

Chapter 13: Support Handstriking and Kicking ............................... 195
Skill and Knowledge 1: Empty Hand and Kicking Support ............... 195
Skill and Knowledge 2: Hand-to-Hand Fighting School ................... 196
Skill and Knowledge 3: The Backup Hand ..................................... 201
Skill and Knowledge 4: Hand Striking Techniques .......................... 205
Skill and Knowledge 5: Kicking Techniques .................................. 207
Skill and Knowledge 6: Basic Knife Support Exercises .................... 210

Chapter 14: Grips, Releases and Counters ................................................ 213
    Strategy and Drill 1: Introduction to the Trapping and Grappling Ranges ............... 213
    Strategy and Drill 2: Grabbing the Knife Hand/Wrist Drills .................................. 215
    Strategy and Drill 3: Circular Pattern Releases ................................................. 217
    Strategy and Drill 4: The Push/Pull Pattern Releases ........................................ 224
    Strategy and Drill 5: Blade Stab Releases ....................................................... 228
    Strategy and Drill 6: The Even-Even Grip Releases .......................................... 232

Chapter 15: Chain of the Knife Drills ....................................................... 241
    Introduction to the Chain Drills ..................................................................... 241
    Chain Drill 1: Torso Stab ............................................................................. 244
    Chain Drill 2: The Upper Arm Destruction ...................................................... 245
    Chain Drill 3: Thigh Slash ............................................................................ 247
    Chain Drill 4: Scoop the Knee ...................................................................... 248
    Chain Drill 5: Finger Slash ........................................................................... 250
    Summary .................................................................................................. 251

Chapter 16: Skill Developing Drills .......................................................... 253
    Introduction .............................................................................................. 253
    Filipino Hubod ........................................................................................... 254
    Torso Attack ............................................................................................. 267
    Knife Sumbrada ......................................................................................... 274
    One Attack Statue Drills .............................................................................. 281
    Give and Take ........................................................................................... 283
    Double Knife Sinawali ................................................................................. 284
    The Throw Away ....................................................................................... 287

Chapter 17: Knife Fighting Combat Scenarios ........................................... 289
    Congress Knife Counter-Knife Combat Training Modules ................................. 290
    Quick Draw: The Knife Acquisition Module .................................................... 291
    The Spartan Street Fighter Module ............................................................... 295
    Chain of the Knife Module ........................................................................... 297
    Alley Cat: Anti-Street Crime Module ............................................................ 302
    Ground Zero: The Knife Ground Fighting Module ............................................ 305
    Do or Die: The Unarmed vs. the Knife Module .............................................. 312
    The British Bastard Mix Module ................................................................... 314
    The S.O.M. - The Special Operations Module ................................................ 317
    In the Final Analysis .................................................................................. 318

# Disclaimer

The study and practice of knife fighting, much like the study of the martial arts, is by nature a dangerous endeavor. You must:

a) Wear proper safety equipment, such as eye protection, gloves, helmets, etc. as your workout requires.
b) Consider your general health. Some of these drills and scenarios are strenuous. Consult your physician before beginning any program.
c) Use the appropriate training knife. The replica should be soft when contact is expected in a training session.
d) Train under the supervision of an authority.
e) Keep emergency medical first aid nearby.

In order for us to be able to share this incredible information with you, we cannot be held responsible for your mistakes. Please be careful!

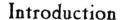

Introduction

# Introduction

Thank you, and welcome to the Year 2000, second edition of *The Foundation: Volume 1: The Knife Fighting Encyclopedia* series. The Foundation is meant to serve as an overall crash course of knife versus knife, and unarmed versus the knife combat in all physical ranges. Subsequent volumes, like *Volume 2: Military Knife Combat* and *Volume 3: Quick Draws and Counters to Quick Draws, Knife Ground Fighting* continue to focus and build on this foundation.

Humans possess both a need for and a fascination with knives. You may find knives nearly anywhere. Every house, restaurant, hot dog stand, mess hall, office break room, airplane and more, has at least one knife. Knives open boxes and cans, hack, shear, shovel, screw, skin. Is it any wonder that knife making and selling as eating cutlery and tools constitute millions of dollars a year in revenue? Aside from that, most people also respect the knife as an instrument of self-defense, crime and combat. The edged weapon stands throughout time as a symbol of war and ugly, close quarter conflict. In its Spartan grip lies the power of life and death. It has made little men big and big men small.

Not including kitchen and tool knives, marketing experts report seven out of 10 knives sold are folding knives, many shaped for fighting. As a result, they play upon this combat mystique. You would be hard pressed to see a photo display in a gun magazine and not find a knife propped nearby, suggesting it as part and parcel of a well thought out self-defense system.

While millions of individuals around the world buy knives, only a miniscule few really know how to use them for self-defense. Even fewer people seek training. Training involves physical exercise, commitment and the development of martial muscle memory. Then one must make a quantum psychological leap to using the knife to maim or kill in self-defense.

Nothing is more diverse and divisive than knife fighting instruction. Stick and gun fighting often appears clear-cut. You get whacked or shot in the head? You're probably down and out. A discerning veteran may easily evaluate hand-to-hand fighting combat. But knife fighting techniques and strategies may seem quite confusing to the novice. What you think will work won't always and vise versa. While some instructors declare knife-arm grabbing techniques impossible, totally untrained citizens frequently execute them successfully during desperate moments. For example, you may find many martial, military, and police instructors who tell their students to never grab the weapon-bearing limb. "It's too fast. You can't catch it!" Five minutes later they are teaching you a technique where you must grab the knife arm. In cases I worked as a cop and in the military, almost all victims of knife attacks survived because they grabbed the weapon-bearing limb as quickly as possible and fought like hell from there.

"Disarms are impossible!" others declare. Then the next day you'll read about the same knife takeaway technique in the local newspaper. How did that impossible fantasy disarm happen? Their lack of real world experience and research prevents these individuals from realizing that disarms occur inside a string of events that usually involves bashing the head of the attacker first, then taking the knife away.

Real world criminal and military history reveals that knife attackers come in all shapes and sizes, with physical skills that span a range from none to superior. In fact, the odds are on your side that the criminal or enemy soldier standing before you is on the lower end of this talent spectrum. Couple that with the general unpredictable chaos of combat, and you have many, many possible scenarios. While anything might happen, I will always endeavor to present to you the best and most plausible tactics. I also feel I must delve a bit more into this continuum-with caveats and explanations-because many things may work depending upon the unique circumstances of the battle. In other words, things that some instructors say can't be done...are probably being done every minute somewhere around the world. My goal is to leave you with knife-fighting savvy. My goal is to inspire you, not confine you.

A knife is a great equalizer, but it is NOT God's gift to equalization. People who sustain cuts or stab wounds do not plummet dead to the floor on contact. While I have investigated a few murders where people did fall and die almost instantly, usually they do not. At best it may take some 15 to 20 seconds for the enemy to bleed out from a very successful bloodline cut. I was privy to an insider state prison video once where an inmate sustained some 200 stab wounds. The victim still fought after 100 stabs! This tells us that a knife fighter not only needs command and mastery of the weapon, but also supplemental skills similar to kick boxing and jujitsu to survive the combat. Someone who has command and mastery of a knife and understands the counters to attack may become a quick and deadly reaper and may leave the fight victorious. Not always unscathed mind you, but alive.

The purpose of this encyclopedia series is to give this edge, this critical knowledge and skill to the Good and the Just, for their defense and the defense of others. The purpose of Volume 1 is to lay a groundwork and foundation upon which we may construct the details.

"Use your knife to save your life!"

## Two slices of the blade

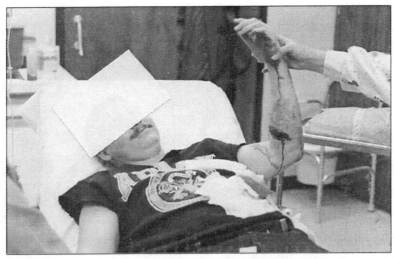

Here, an unathletic, chubby college kid took a slash during a traffic altercation with an angry driver. The kid disarmed his attacker and drove six blocks to the hospital. He walked into the ER smiling and calm. This photo was taken before any medication. Events like this blow big holes in the expert's theory that, "one knife slash renders a person into debilitating shock."

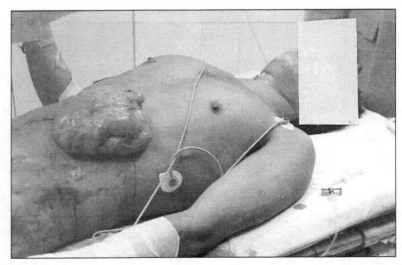

No, that is not a brain resting on this man's stomach. Here, just one quick knife flick tore the muscle lining, and his intestines exploded outward from his body's natural internal pressure.

*The Author*

Chapter 1

# Knife Fighting Encounters

## Three Types of Knife Fighting Encounters:

Crime and history tell us that an edged-weapon encounter can happen anywhere. A street, an elevator, a school yard, a kitchen, a church, a prison, inside a car...anywhere. Despite the environmental variety, there are only three basic knife fighting encounters. As you proceed through this encyclopedia you will learn specific fighting stances and techniques to utilize. All the training in this encyclopedia works through these three basic scenarios:

1) knife vs. knife;
2) you are armed, and the opponent or opponents are not;
3) you are unarmed, the opponent or opponents are.

## Encounter 1: Knife vs. Knife

### Military knife vs. knife fighting

In war, or in peace-keeping, soldiers with a do-or-die mission might find knife vs. knife fighting an unescapable event, forcing them into a blade-to-blade encounter.

### Law enforcement knife vs. knife fighting

For a police officer, knife-to-knife fighting should be avoided if at all possible! Handguns, impact weapons, spray, or even evasive footwork and a "officer needs assistance" radio call for backup are better alternatives. But in my opinion, if an officer is down to fighting with a backup lock-blade or a belt utility knife, it is probably an unavoidable life or death situation. The officer needs blood and guts survival skills.

## Citizen knife vs. knife fighting

Perhaps if you are a citizen defending your life, or the lives of your family, friends or strangers, you might be compelled to take on the grave risk of knife vs. knife.

No matter who you are—soldier, cop, or citizen—if you carry a knife, you need to know how to use it, from A to Z.

## All encounters are dangerous

Would you enter into any encounter more alert, more concerned, more prepared, if you knew that a knife or gun is possibly involved?

There is an old police expression: "Every police encounter involves a loaded gun." This is because the police themselves carry the loaded gun into the situation. The same holds true if you are carrying a knife. Whether or not you show it, use it, or it is taken away from you, if you are armed, then the potential for a knife fight is there. Be responsible. Be alert. Be concerned. Be prepared.

## Encounter 2: Your Knife vs. the Unarmed

Being forced into fighting an unarmed attacker has its advantages, providing you know how to work a blade and can guard against disarms. This encyclopedia will show you how to prepare and overcome the opponent.

## Encounter 3: You Are Unarmed, and the Enemy Has a Knife

If your opponent has the knife and you have none, avoiding the fight and escaping is the paramount plan. But if you can't flee, you still have survival options. This encyclopedia will explain them in detail.

# Chapter 2

# Basic Knife Fighting Strategies

### Strategy 1: Overcoming the Fear of Knife Fighting

*"Unit 111...respond to a violent domestic disturbance with knives..."*

*"Unit 111...respond to fighting subject under the influence of drugs in a restaurant at..."*

I am often asked if I experience fear when, as a police officer, I am dispatched to a violent domestic disturbance, fight call, shots fired call, or any number of police assignments. People frequently tell me that they would be paralyzed with fear when put in my position, or have admitted that they have experienced confrontations of many sorts, and have frozen. "How do you do it?" "Do you feel fear?" As a 23-year police vet and a holder of five black belts, do people assume I am fearless?

To engage in an oxymoron, I would become afraid of myself if I did not taste fear! Of course, I feel the inbred animal instinct of fear, like most people. Fear can be both a motivator and a savior, tipping off your adrenalin, motivating you to train for emergencies, or warning you away from problem areas.

While an adrenalin rush can sometimes be your friend, it can also be your enemy. It gives you "tunnel vision," can steal your breath, and the impending adrenalin "dump" can virtually disable you—leaving you a shaking, energy-drained mess. Ask any police officer who is required to fill out paperwork after a street fight, how shaky his or her handwriting is. There are times, however, when soldiers, police officers and normal citizens must overcome their natural fears, and act.

To differing degrees, everyone faces adversity, stress and confrontation in everyday challenges. Normal people experience "normal" fear, that is to say fear that is relative and logical to the predicament. Abnormal or illogical fear becomes a neurosis or worse—a psychosis. For example, all people have a natural fear or respect of heights, yet this fear should not inhibit someone from using an elevator or prohibit them from looking out a window from inside a skyscraper. But how does one overcome the normal fears, and specifically, fear of verbal and physical confrontation—the fear of fighting, or even worse, fear of knife fighting? It is one thing to have a healthy fear of the knife, but yet another to freeze like a babbling idiot while you and your family are carved up by an untrained lunatic.

### "Just concentrate?"
It is so easy for a self-defense instructor, or any teacher to throw out terms like, "Focus!" "Concentrate!" "Think positive," as if those commands will automatically overcome all of these "fears of fighting." I am often reminded of the school boy who is not answering his math questions correctly. The teacher orders him, "Okay, Johnny, CONCENTRATE!" The boy picks up his pencil and contorts his face. Scowling, he tightens all his facial muscles to "concentrate!" Now, tightening those forehead muscles and severely frowning has absolutely nothing to do with the mechanics of concentration, nor does it aid in any way the steps involved in seeking the mathematical solution. More than likely, he will continue to fail math and have a tired face to boot!

### Concentration is one part of the equation
What is more important, is actually fleshing out the ways of focusing, concentrating, and creating positive energy in manageable, attainable, goal-oriented steps. Let's dissect these words as they specifically relate to the fear of fighting.

1) Focus: One should focus in on the specific goal at hand.
2) Concentration: One should concentrate on executing the specific steps of the goal.
3) Repetition: One should practice these specific steps, dissolving them into one's muscle memory and mentality.
4) Positive energy: One finds solace,

confidence and enlightenment, in knowing she or he has prepared appropriately for the situation.

So the equation reads:

*Focus + concentration + repetition = positive mentality (confidence), and confidence lessens fear.*

## Concentrate on executing goal specific steps

The act or "art" of fighting in a street survival situation is a physical action. Simply put, it is very much like an episode or a task in a physical job or sporting event. A person's size, strength, coordination, speed, and mentality all come into play. The success of a knife slash, a punch or throw, is really not unlike skills a linebacker utilizes to stop a play, or someone perfecting a golf swing, or holding a two-by-four into position and hammering a nail, or cutting a straight line with a buzz saw.

So let's look at a sport's task to better understand a fighting task. Let's say we are observing a baseball pitcher in a World Series game. He is "goal-oriented," and very concerned with winning, and as he throws each pitch, his mind is full of thoughts like, "I must win this game! I must win for the team, the fans! Thousands of people depend on me. I need the play-off money for my house mortgage! I must

win!" Now these are extremely positive thoughts, but are they of a type that are a distraction against success?

Let's look at a "goal-specific" pitcher. He is on the mound with the exact same pressures and the same goal-oriented, winning mentality. He's got fans, and a mortgage, too, but he is more concerned with the specific tasks at hand. Instead of thinking about winning to pay the mortgage, he concerns himself with accurately placing his fingers on the seam of the ball, checking to see where the catcher's mitt is placed in the strike zone, and other goal-specific tasks that he has practiced thousands of times. He is not so much concerned with winning the game, but concentrating on throwing the best fast ball for the moment that he possibly can. Pitch by pitch. Act by act. "By the yard, life is hard, by the inch, it's a cinch."

Which of the two pitchers do you think is more likely to succeed? Theoretically, the goal-specific pitcher has the best chance. Throw the best pitch each and every time, and winning the game should take care of itself. Obsessing about winning, and the unrelated issues surrounding winning, actually distracts you from concentrating and executing the very things you need to do to win!

How does this relate to fighting and self-defense? When you must square off against an opponent, you must not let goal-oriented thoughts like, "Oh my God, I must win this fight; I will die if I don't," overcome you. "I have a wife and kids at home. What will their lives be without me? What will the dentist cost if I lose a tooth? Will I need a plastic surgeon when it's over?...etc." Even if these words aren't articulated precisely in the brain, they construct the catalyst for sheer fear.

Instead, you should be thinking only goal-specific problem solving. He is wearing thick glasses. I'll bat them off! A good kick to the shin or knee will slow him down! Let's see how well he protects his eyes. He sure keeps his "on-guard" arms low! There's that opening again!

Approach a fight in scientific pieces like this, and "winning" will take care of itself.

Now, how did our pitcher wind up in the World Series in the first place? By applying all these principles and by repetition. How did the carpenter become a craftsman? The same way. They repeated the process of proper technique thousands of times, breaking down and perfecting each bit and breath. The ball-player did it in practice and in real life, and as we all know real-life experience is the best of all teachers. So that tells us that we must spend a portion of our survival training in an environment that is as real as constructurally possible, to best inoculate ourselves for the real thing.

There was once an oriental martial arts master who said, "One should avoid all fights, but if one has to fight, one should simply relax and enjoy oneself." It is somewhat comical to many martial artists. We get the joke. To others, it might be hard to imagine, but some level of relaxation, along with some level of excitement, or fear if you will, are required to survive.

Relaxed, limber muscles facilitate speed. Tense muscles, like the facial expression of our student I mentioned earlier trying to concentrate on his math, have nothing to do with the mechanics of winning a fight. Tightened muscles look great in photos and in the movies, but they are detrimental to your survival success.

How do you possibly bring relaxation into an encounter? If you study fighting, if you drill realistic repetitions, you will find solace in that you have prepared as best you can, and you will have confidence that you have a chance. Did I say this before...confidence lessens fear?

Look at it this way. If you were only a fair marksman, and holding a gun in your hand, you had to walk down a dark and dangerous alley, that gun would give you a certain level of confidence, wouldn't it! You would feel as though you had a chance to survive! Well, you carry weapons with you every day, your hands, elbows, feet, knees, body weight, your savvy and intensity, etc.; all are incredible weapons! Learn how to "shoot" them!

"How long before I can become a good, confident fighter?" I am often asked by potential students. That would be like asking a tennis coach, "How long must I train before I will start winning tennis competitions?" It depends on you, and what you bring to the table. There is no quick fix to becoming a good empty hand fighter. At best, I will tell you three basic principles:

a)  attack the knees,
b)  tangle the arms,
c)  attack the head...and not necessarily in that order! But that's the subject of another encyclopedia.

"How long before I can become a good, confident knife fighter?"

You must bring to the table these same physical skills. Then take on all the alterations and work involved directly with fighting with the knife. Again, there is no quick fix. I can add some basic principles of knife fighting mentality:

a)  steel yourself to the fact that you are going to get cut, so minimize the psychological damage,
b)  make maximum use of your physical skills and environment,

c)  cut to disarm the opponent as a strategy and priority.

Through the years, I have gone through many phases of fear about knife fighting. At first, I desperately feared the blade. Then, after I trained wisely, I became confident and perhaps, over-cocky. Then the next phase hit me where I lost this machismo recklessness. Instead, I learned to concentrate on each task at hand. Therein lies the secret to survival.

I hope I will always be stimulated by normal fear. Now, I realize that all my years in police work and the martial arts cannot guarantee my survival, safety, or protection against injury in an empty hand or knife fight. But fear has prodded me into proper training and has given me a fighting chance. I now have some solace, hope and confidence, and CONFIDENCE LESSENS FEAR! This is my hope for you.

## Strategy 2: The Elements of Surprise, Shock, and Fight or Flight

Working to overcome the basic fears of hand-to-hand or knife fighting, does not guarantee you can overcome the physiological effects of surprise, shock or the fight or flight instinct.

### Surprise

The element of surprise has always been a superior military and survival tactic. Some of the finest armies, soldiers, police officers and fighters have all fallen prey to the guerrilla attack-element of surprise.

To illustrate this, on the streets of America, more than half the successful knife-attacks upon the police in this country are surprise attacks. Case after case, officers have been jumped from the shadows, or cut and stabbed by positioning themselves too close to a contacted person. In the day-to-day business of police work, officers must step precariously close to scores of people, and the risk level is many times undetectable, and almost unavoidable.

A once-wounded officer said:

*"You think if someone is going to attack you with a knife you will do some flashy thing, like a takedown you learned from the Academy or something. But, it happens so fast! From out of nowhere, the guy pulled a knife and slashed open my face."*

This officer's statement, which belittles Academy training, and henceforth, all training, creates a sense of hopelessness for people learning self defense. "What real good will it do?" they might ask. It actually speaks much more about the element of surprise in a particular set of circumstances. The officer was a victim of a surprise attack. Do not let the universal strategy of surprise, which can defeat even Superman, confuse you about your need to train. Even Mike Tyson can get coldcocked out of the blue! That doesn't mean all Tyson's boxing training is worthless. If the guy's coldcock misses, watch out!

Minus these forced dynamics of officer and criminal confrontations, regular citizens are not usually attacked in this sudden, surprise manner, though it can and certainly has happened. Usually civilian encounters heat up for a variety of emotional reasons, and then a knife is displayed; or it is displayed for a psychological tool to shock you, force you to do something, or rob you.

A subject wanting the advantage of surprise will usually require one or more of the following:

a)  quickdraw skill,
b)  concealed or reverse grip tactics,
c)  some athletic skills,
d)  knowledge of the environment,

e) aggressive commitment,

f) knowledge about you or people like you.

There are ways to help defeat or lessen the element of surprise:

a) common knowledge that certain circumstances and neighborhoods are more dangerous than others. For example, mall parking lot robbery rates are higher than say, bowling alley lots, or dentist office lots. Christmas season mall parking lot robbery rates are even higher.

With some common sense, you can "escalate" your awareness levels. Avoid passing places where someone could be hiding. Have your keys out and ready. Look underneath your car as you approach it. Look inside before you get in. Circle your car once, and see what "flushes out" from behind or nearby parked cars. Look around before you open the trunk. Do you see the awareness strategy? You can help make the element of surprise less debilitating.

b) train in fighting techniques so much that they become muscle memory. Your element of surprise reactions can contain survival reflexes.

After the initial display and attack, the element of surprise becomes the element of shock.

**Shock**

As surprise fades, next you will most likely be shocked that you have been attacked. You may or may not be cut. Regardless, you will still be shocked to some degree. In the shock phase, the most common encounter is the face off encounter. You have stepped back from the surprise attack, cut or not, and are now face-to-face with the attacker.

**Fight or flight**

If your mentality is right, Shock must now fade into the decision-making process of fight or flight, and quickly! Experts in human and animal behavior say that "fight or flight" is an instinctive behavior. If you can escape the knife fighter, ESCAPE! If you can't, you must fight for your life, and this is where your training comes in.

**The Three F's of Fear:**

1) Freeze (or shock)
2) Flight
3) Fight

**Then More Options:**

1) Posturing
2) Submission

(See Volume 2 of the Encyclopedia series for an in-depth study on these topics.)

## Strategy 3: Armed vs. Armed Progression Strategy

When suddenly confronted with a knife fight and you have a knife, consider these options:

1) Yell or scream to create a disturbance and attract attention and witnesses.

2) If you can't...stay as far away from his blade as possible with evasive foot-work. In this evasion period, reach for your "distance weapons" you might be carrying, such as guns, expandable batons, mace, or search your environment for shields like a chair or stick. A stick is a long-range weapon and can help keep the opponent at bay. Seek out significant things to throw. Start talking and bargaining for escape or closure, such as his flight or his surrender.

3) If you can't...draw your knife. Keep talking about his flight, his surrender, or even his maiming and death as a result of this inevitable knife-to-knife encounter.

4) Keep studying your environment for possible escape.

5) With a strong side, knife forward, stance, engage in combat with the opponent. Your primary goal should be to cut the opponent's knife out of his hand. If he is foolish enough to fight you from a rear hand knife stance, your closest target will be his "foolish" cover arm he serves up to "protect" his knife. Cut it to ribbons. But! Should a more appropriate target suddenly appear, such as a long-range kick at you, economy of motion dictates that you strike out at this target. Consider the density of his clothing versus your blade. Assess his conditioning. It is said that, at this confrontational flashpoint, many attackers will flee when they see your blade.

6) Using all your footwork skills, strategies, blade attacking, blocking, disarming, backup hand and foot fighting muscle memory learned from this encyclopedia and support tape series, fight for your life with explosive intensity!

7) If you injure or kill this opponent, remember to explain to the authorities you were in fear for your life and fought the opponent not to kill him but to **STOP** him. Be friendly and cooperative with arriving authorities, but consider getting legal counsel before making any statements. Beware, in many states, even "first-blush" verbal statements that are now called "excitable utterances," can be used against you.

## Strategy 4: Armed vs. Unarmed Progression Strategy

When you are being attacked and you have a knife, your opponent does not, and the opponent is not yielding, consider these options:

1) Yell and scream to create a disturbance and attract attention and witnesses.
2) At a safe distance, prominently display your blade, in an effort to discourage the opponent.
3) Use whatever verbal skills you have to discourage the opponent. Try to insure that witnesses hear your pleadings.
4) Strike a fighting stance. Many fighters up against an unarmed attacker will stand so that their strong side/knife hand is back, using their free arm and hand up-front to guard against "suicide" disarm charges. Other fighters may choose a strong side forward stance. If you properly train using the disarming techniques in this encyclopedia, you will be aware of what disarms the opponent might try.
5) Try to maneuver your unarmed opponent into a position where:

   a) he cannot get access to objects in the environment he can use to shield himself, wrap his arms or acquire things to throw at you;

   b) there is an escape route for him to take. Verbalize this procedure loudly so that witnesses can see you are offering the opponent every opportunity to save himself.

6) Using all of your footwork skills, strategies, blade attacking, blocking, disarming, backup hand and foot fighting muscle learned from this encyclopedia and support tape series, fight for your life with explosive intensity!
7) If you injure or kill this opponent, remember to explain to the authorities you were in fear for your life and fought the opponent not to kill him but to **STOP** him. You are in an especially vulnerable position, legally. You were armed, and he was not. As stated before in the previous section, beware of saying the wrong thing for verbal statements might be used against you. More on this later.

## Strategy 5: Unarmed and Fighting the Knife Progression Strategy

When suddenly confronted with a knife fight and you are unarmed, consider these options:

1) Run and yell or scream to create a disturbance and attract attention and witnesses.
2) If you can't...stay as far away from the knife as possible with evasive foot-work. Now is the time for mace, pepper spray style weapons if you have them.
3) If you can't...check out your environment for potential protection, and/or weapons against the knife.
4) If you can't...consider wrapping your jacket or shirt on a arm to protect you against the blade.
5) If you can't...verbalize words of cooperation and bargaining for a chance to escape unhurt.
6) If you can't...turn the outsides of your forearms out to the opponent, protecting your softer muscle and major blood veins on the insides of your arms. Your hands can protect your neck.
7) If still attacked...attempt evasion and resign yourself that this encounter will most likely result in you being cut. Prepare for this and work to minimize these cuts.
8) If still attacked...fight like hell. Attempt blocks, hand and foot strikes and disarms. Go down fighting. You may never have to go!
9) If you injure or kill this opponent, remember to explain to the authorities you were in fear for your life and fought the opponent not to kill him but to **STOP** him. You are in the best of legal positions here, but will have to explain:

a) why you didn't and couldn't run,
b) any overkill stabs or slashes you inflicted,
c) why you didn't just run when you got the knife from the aggressor.

It might be wise to make the briefest of explanations and acquire a lawyer.

## Strategy 6: The Mad Rush

One of the common attack encounters one faces is the "mad rush." The mad rush is a sudden dash at you and:

1) it could be crazed,
2) it could be calm and precise,
3) it could come knife first,
4) it could come first in the form of:

    a) kicking and punching, then the knife-attack,
    b) trapping your limbs down for a knife-attack,
    c) grappling in the form of tackle, then a knife-attack.

The mad rush can come at any time during the surprise attack or the face-off encounter. Here are some counter-strategies.

### 1) Maintain a safe distance

Understand that it is physically impossible to respond to a split-second, close-quarter attack. Your reaction time takes a micro second longer than the initial attack. Keep a safe distance to react, and that safe distance is relative to the situation. This concerns itself with people and geography. Keep a safe distance from suspicious people, and obviously armed people. You should keep a safe distance from objects like walls and columns, and anything that might conceal suspicious or obviously dangerous people.

And what is a safe distance? A safe distance can be defined as a distance at which you can:

    a) escape without injury,
    b) successfully pull your weapon and counter-attack.

To give you one idea of what a safe distance might be, consider this "mad rush" police test. Scientific trials have been conducted on an unobstructed straight run. If a police officer is rushed by a knife-attacker in such a manner, it takes from 19 to 21 feet for officers to pull a pistol from a open holster and shoot the attacker. Twenty-one feet!

Stress plays a part. In this scenario, stress can come from:

    a) simply being on the receiving end of a mad rush,
    b) the mad, mean or cool psychotic facial expression of the rusher,
    c) the manner of the scream accompanying the rush.

Officers in the act of pulling their gun under this stress sometimes pull with two hands (one on the holster—one on the gun handle), this despite all their one-hand-draw range training.

This double dip at the gun exposes their torso to attack. Often they backpeddle (run backward) and quickly stumble over any object in the terrain, or even over their own two feet.

Remember this stat, 21 feet, when you are practicing the quickdraw of your knife, because the dynamics of drawing a knife are very similar. Now imagine if your knife is buried in your boot or some other covered location.

## 2) Evasive footwork

One way to defeat a mad rush attack and buy more reaction time is to do something you might see weekly on television or in any athletic stadium. The skills used by a football receiver wishing to trick a defender, or a soccer player wishing to confuse the opponent, can be utilized. Dodging, backpeddling, faking, cutting to the right or left at the last second, can trick the opponent and buy precious quickdraw weapon time, or escape. So, to counter the mad rush, you must practice:

a) dodging,
b) faking,
c) cutting,
d) backpeddling to draw a weapon, or turning and running.

## 3) Use the environment

Strategies against the mad rush can include use of the environment or the terrain. You can position yourself so that something, a fence, a rock, furniture, whatever, is between you and the attacker.

## 4) Develop muscle memory responses

Using the methods taught in the encyclopedia, develop and practice into muscle memory the responses to the mad rush scenarios.

I have produced a one hour Congress Knife Fighting video called "Combat The Mad Rush," that teaches empty hand vs. knife and knife vs. knife options against this style of attack. These options include a lot of grappling.

## Strategy 7: The Law and You, After the Encounter

How you act after the fight can effect criminal and civil investigation. There are two things you can do after the knife fight:

1) Flee. You can elude identification, as some experts openly tell you to do because of the expenses, hassles, punishments and general flakiness of our legal system. If you escape, you will exist with what I call the "fugitive factor" your whole life. Your neck will always be a little stiff from looking over your shoulder.
2) You can report the fight to the police. Get a good lawyer.

I will talk to you from my experience and knowledge as a detective and patrol officer. Your knife fighting actions will be siphoned through many legal filters that will decide what, if any, criminal or civil prosecution you might face.

### 1) The physical events of the fight
In a thorough investigation by the police, a step-by-step chronicle of the fight should be constructed.

### 2) The famous "Could you have run?" Filter
This question has been known to have been asked by attorneys of both sides. If you could have turned and run before, or at any second during the fight, you will probably have to explain why you didn't.

### 3) The wounds
The wounds will be scrutinized. Do they suggest "overkill." Remember what is not overkill to a person fighting for their life, can be overkill to a "Sunday Morning Quarterback," or someone ignorant to the realities of fighting. Are the wounds consistent with the reported events?

### 4) Blood spatter and blood stains
Blood shedding will be, or at least should be, scrutinized to see if it is consistent with the events of the fight and wounds.

### 5) Utterances and statements
What you said or didn't say, and how you acted, when the police first arrived can make a big difference. Everyone knows the famous Bernard Goetz utterance "You don't look too bad, here's another (bullet)." You should be friendly and cooperative when the police arrive. State clearly, "He attacked me, and I want to press charges against him." Then in a friendly and apologetic manner advise them you think it would be wise for you to consult with a lawyer ASAP.

**6) Knife mystique and ignorance**
The cultural misunderstandings of the knife and its manifestations.

**7) Your background**
Are you an upstanding citizen? Has this happened to you before? Have you held a steady job and raised a family?

**8) Your opponent's background**

**9) Witness recollections**
What has the witness perceived, and what will the witness say?

**10) Investigator skill and prejudices**
What are the experience, workload, predilections and personalities of the detectives assigned to investigate the matter.

**11) The investigator's supervisor's priorities, skill and prejudices**
The supervisors can exert influence and control upon the investigation.

**12) The prosecutor's skill and prejudices**
What are the experience, workload, predilections, personalities and politics of the prosecutors' supervisors,

**13) The prosecutor's supervisor's priorities, skill and prejudices**
The supervisors can exert influence and control upon the investigation.

**14) The socio-economics of the community members involved**

**15) The past criminal history of the area and/or the whole city or county**

**16) The defense attorney's skill and local influence with the D.A.**
How good and connected is the defense? Some obnoxious attorneys are hated and receive no cooperation from the D.A.'s office. Some are friendly, with working relationships that promote good flow of information and problem-solving.

**17) Special interest groups**
Are there any anti-gang, racially-motivated, or public safety organizations that can worm their political stance into the facts of your situation?

**18) Past jury performances on similar cases in and out of your locality**

**19 and ...) Many additional factors.**

Your fight will be filtered through most, and sometimes all, of these considerations before you'll find out if you are in serious trouble or "no-billed" and vindicated. Just because you didn't get indicted on a criminal charge doesn't mean you won't get sued in civil court. That process is also expensive.

I tell you to run from a knife fight for two reasons, one is the deadliness of the blade, the other is that big, complicated crapshoot we call the criminal justice system. Often it works well, but sometimes it doesn't...and that sometimes might just be with you.

But at the flashpoint of the blade, you or yours may be killed. "Tried by 12, or carried by six?" Jury or pallbearers? Pick the 12.

I am currently a private investigator in the State of Texas. I am a certified blood spatter expert, graduate of several violent death and assault schools. With this and all my years experience in law enforcement and the martial arts, I am a legal expert on knife fighting. I have testified in Federal and State courts on weaponry and knives, and I can testify in your trial about knife-related and self defense issues if deemed appropriate. Contact me.

In the study of the art, the way and the science of knife fighting, I will show you many techniques and strategies from first contact to kill. It is up to you, the situation, your ethics and morality to decide when you bail out. It also is important to learn what someone can ruthlessly do to you!

## Summary

### "In the service of" attacks

Usually it is the soldier, the police and security officer who are victimized routinely by a complete surprise knife-attack. There are three basic psychological phases involved with being victimized by a sudden attack:

1) element of surprise
2) element of shock
3) fight or flight

### Non-service attacks

While regular people can also be victimized by surprise knife-attacks, they are usually confronted by knives after emotional or "criminal" situations like threats, kidnapping, rape or robbery.

### The common denominator encounters

Service or not, after surviving the surprise attack, these physical encounters are the most common in knife fighting.

1) face-off armed vs. armed
2) face-off, you are unarmed vs. the armed
3) face-off, you are armed vs. the unarmed
4) face-off and the "mad rush"

### During the fight

Use the conditioning, skills and wit taught in this encyclopedia to survive.

### After the fight

Be aware of the many legal considerations of your actions.

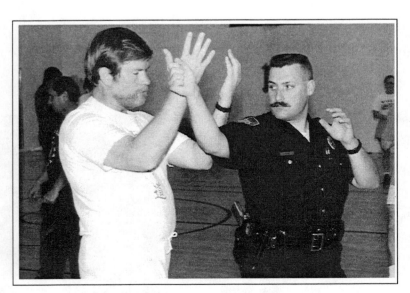

Here, my student, Officer Don Lane practices in his uniform to feel the weight and constraints he will feel in the real world.

You need "in and out" footwork skills.

You need "quickdraw" skills.

1

3

2

4

You must use tools in your environment.

1

2

# Chapter 3

# Knife Selection

### Selection 1: The Training Knife

There are five types of training knives. Selecting the best knife for training will depend on your proposed drill and practitioner safety.

1) a soft knife usually made of cut-out foam or rubber
2) a soft knife that can hinge open like a folding knife
3) a dull, or no-edge wooden knife
4) a dull, or no-edge metal knife
5) a sharp-edged metal knife

### Training knife 1: The soft knife

The soft knife is used when there is an emphasis on stabbing or hard-striking your partner. It can also be used in groundfighting drills when a harder blade could injure you or your partner during the randori-style wrestling. A rubber knife, usually more stout than a sponge or bendable knife, is great for knife sparring.

You can acquire such rubber knives from martial arts supply stores and in some cases-even toy stores. You can also get a sheet of foam and cut out a knife shape, or use plumber's pipe-covering insulation. It is advisable to use a shape that is the same or as similar as possible to the knife you will really use.

Despite the fact your training knife may be rubber, you can hurt yourself or others. The harder blades can bruise and injure forearms or other body parts. Rubber knife strikes can sting and bruise. Always wear eye protection.

### Training knife 2: The soft knife with a hinge

The hinge or folder knife replica is an important piece in modern-day knife training. Many people carry folders now, be they "clip-its" or just "deep-pocket" carries. A carrier must practice his or her quick-draw, which can be done in the air with the real blade. The next level of quick-draw training comes in the draw and stab or slash phase. This is where the soft knife with a hinge comes in. Practitioners should be able to draw and attack under pressure, while wrestling an opponent. This practice knife lets the person reach into a pocket, unfold and stab or slash in the close-quarter chaos of a real struggle and groundfight. These can be made from styrofoam and a small rivet. I have used rubber kitchen measuring spoons that pivot on a bar. You can tape off all but one spoon, and open the remaining spoon in training to simulate opening a folder.

### Training knife 3: The wooden knife

The wooden knife, aside from its esoteric grain patterns and shapes, is good when a solid substance is in order. You may wish to practice push/pull disarms and you need a solid blade to push against, or you may

just have a more realistic approach to training.

You can acquire such wooden knives from martial arts supply stores. You can also cut them out of pine or other woods yourself. I have seen many exotic wood knives in interesting shapes. It is advisable to use a shape that is the same or as similar as possible to the knife you will really use.

### Training knife 4: The dull-edged metal knife

The metal knife, with its inherent flash, adds more of a realistic feel and look to training. It has all the scare and no cutting edge. You can acquire these knives from martial art stores. Some people practice with dull kitchen butter knives with the serrated edges filed or taped off. Others cut the shapes out of thin metal and create a handle with wrapped cord, rubber or cloth.

### Training knife 5: Sharp-edged metal knife

If you practice throwing a knife, you need a real one. You must also practice slashing, hacking or stabbing techniques on or into targets, bags, trees, whatever, and you will need a sharp point and edge. If you practice reality in your slashing, stabbing or your knife-exiting skills—that is twisting and/or yanking your already embedded blade from bags, trees, butchered animal meats, etc.—you need a real blade. You can acquire these in retail knife and martial arts operations.

## Selection 2: The Fighting Knife

Let me start by saying that I am not going to tell you what your favorite fighting knife should be. Of all the utility knives, fantasy blades, war daggers, etc., you must choose one for yourself.

People will choose knives for their personal preference, based upon their fashion, their background, their beliefs. In this sense, these knives give them power and confidence. I know a special operations soldier who carried an old-fashioned Bowie knife into the Vietnam swamp combat, when other "smarter" blades were certainly optional. But now my friend cannot carry this favorite on the streets of New York! He carries a folder clipped to his pocket.

But there are some knives that need to be hung over the fireplace for show! Before you decide what to keep on your person and what should hang in a shadow box on the mantle, here are basic fighting knife points worth consideration.

### Fighting knife selection point 1: Over-all knife weight and size

1)  Does the knife "feel" good in your hand? Most experts break down a knife into two categories, blade weight and handle weight. More importantly, workout with it, and test it. Stab it into various substances. Slice it across various substances. Also, take it hunting and camping. Dress out some game. Now, does it feel as good as it works?

2)  Then you must select a type of knife that is practical for your travels. Your jungle knife can't be carried on Daytona beach in the summer. Your little belt-line-carry knife will be buried deep under layers of zippered clothing in an Alaskan winter.

### Fighting knife selection point 2: The handle

The handle or grip, should be sized properly and therefore fit in your hand comfortably. It should be made out of, and textured to offer, a sturdy grip when under the test of sweat, blood and oil. Some of the new checkered, patterned, lighter plastic and rubber handles are wiser carries than the prettier, smoother and heavier models. I have worked with some wooden handle knives than turned into a "wet bar of soap" when spattered with hunted game blood.

### Fighting knife selection point 3: The hilt guard

The guard is on a knife for three reasons:

1)  to prevent your hand from sliding up onto the blade if you stab something,

2)  to prevent another sharp edge from attacking your hand. They were

invented to guard you and catch incoming swords,

3) and aesthetics. Beautifully constructed and composed guards and hilts can add to the overall aesthetic shape and feel of a knife.

**Fighting knife selection point 4: The actual blade**

Make sure the blade offers sharpened edges where you like them. Some hunting knives have working hooks for game dressing. These hooks will slow you down in survival fighting. You cannot have your fighting knife hooked into the anatomy of your opponent. There are three basic kinds of fighting knife blades:

1) double edge—both sides are sharp
2) single edge—one side is sharp
3) false-edge or single and a half edge— that is, one side is sharp, the back outer half of the blade is also sharp. This allows for better penetration into the target. Some false-edge critics claim that a false edge weakens the end of the blade.

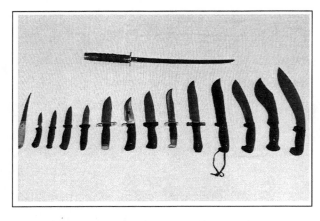

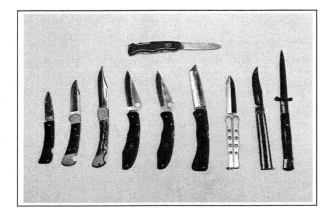

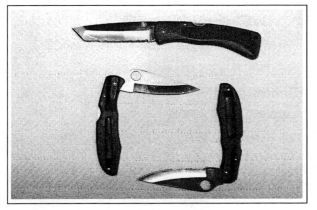

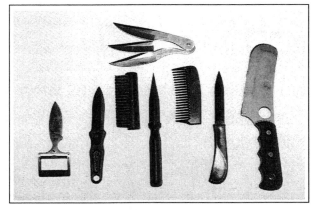

## Knife fighting selection point 5: The pommel

Folding knives do not usually have the practical concern of pommel fighting features and designs. Fixed blades often do.

I started my study in the martial arts and knife fighting in 1973 in an Ed Parker Kenpo Karate school in Irving, Texas. The school had several Gil Hibbon model fighting knives we trained with. One of its unique features was a harsh-edged pommel. It worked especially well in the reverse grip, where the sharpened pommel led the way in punching style attacks.

But a pommel doesn't have to be sharp for it to have impact value. There are knives with rounded ball-shaped pommels, or other exotic designs. Whatever the design, the pommel can be another attack feature of a fighting knife and something for you to consider in your knife-selection strategies.

## Knife fighting selection point 6: Thongs

Some knives have a hole in the handle for a thong. This thong, be it cord, chain or leather, can loop your hand and/or wrist to prevent your loss of the knife during a fight.

As a uniformed military police officer, I had to wear a lanyard from my shoulder to the butt of my handgun when in my Class A uniform. Two times this lanyard proved a useful asset. Once, an MP was knocked over in a fight and fell some eight feet on a slanted field. Ordinarily, his .45 would have flown wild from his hand, but was within retractable reach by hauling in the lanyard. Secondly, I recall a time when an MP was shot. He lost the grip on his gun and was knocked off his feet. He was able to recover what would have been a lost handgun by way of the lanyard to further protect himself. A thong on a knife handle can achieve the same safety net.

## Knife selection point 7: What I carry

I am not trying to endorse my favorite knives over any others. There are just as many practical fighting knives on the market as there are fantasy knives. I love the look, shape and feel of knives, and it is always very difficult for me to settle in on ownership.

But, I carry a Cold Steel brand, folding Tanto knife in the pocket of my police uniform every workday, and also in appropriate off-duty "big-pocket" wear. I have chosen this style knife from my own personal and esoteric love in the Japanese Martial Arts. Then I carry a smaller Spiderco for concealed off-duty wear.

I also love to work out with, and carry when I can, a simple and inexpensive, fixed-blade, Colt knife. Its slight overall curve fits my hand and feels perfect. The grip offers "guard-like" protection with a molded low-side curve that builds into a metal half guard. I prefer knives with half-guards on the bottom and no guard on the top. This way, the back of the blade is flat so I can work my thumb on and off of the blade for a variety of tasks. I prefer to have the outer back part of the blade, down toward the tip, sharpened for all the blade twisting attack techniques I like to practice.

When I teach classes and seminars, I use a host of different sized and shaped knives.

## Hilt guard case study 1

I recall a police case I worked where a man was brutally stabbed and left for dead at a party. The suspect fled out a back door and through neighborhood yards. We searched for him and routinely scoured the bushes, trash cans etc., in the neighborhood, for a discarded knife because often, suspects discard their weapons so as not to be caught with incriminating evidence. But our 40 minute search was called off when we heard from the hospital ER. Nurses had recovered the knife! It was caught and hooked up in the baggy clothing of the victim, thanks to the hilt/guard of the knife.

In this case, the suspect had successfully removed the blade from the victim's wound canal, but couldn't clear the weapon from the victim's clothing, which was nothing more than a flannel shirt and sweater. Later, I examined this knife and observed that the hilt was not excessively large.

## Hilt guard case study 2

I responded once to a fresh crime scene of an armed robbery of a convenience store clerk, who had been stabbed multiple times by a suspect. I organized a quick search of the area for this suspect. It was evident by a blood trail leaving the store, that during the robbery/assault, the suspect must have cut himself. A patrol officer encountered an uncooperative person a few blocks away. As we had anticipated of the suspect, this hostile person had a telltale combination of a cut on his strong-side hand, and a folding pocket knife in a jacket pocket.

The pocket knife had no hilt as most don't, and when the suspect stabbed the clerk with enough force to penetrate the clerk's clothing and skin, his hand slid right up on the blade, deeply cutting his finger.

Months later, he was convicted on several points. One was victim ID. Second, his own blood was recovered from the scene. (No "O.J. Simpson" DNA debate here!) The suspect's knife had the victim's dried blood on the blade and inside the handle. And of course, photographs were introduced of the cut on the suspect's hand, which explained why the suspect's blood was found on the scene. I had to testify why so many people accidentally cut themselves while stabbing someone using a knife without a guard.

The moral of these two hilt guard case studies is, select a knife with a small hilt or even a half hilt to prevent:

1) it becoming tangled in obstacles. If you are forced to fight more than one opponent, you cannot have your knife hooked up in an opponent's clothing.
2) your hand from slipping up on the blade. You need some type of a hilt to save your hand.

**WARNING!**

After I extracted a wicked two-inch splinter from the forearm of Mr. John Drew in a Monroe, LA seminar in October of 1997, I decided that wooden knives can be very dangerous to train with. I envisioned what that splinter would do in someone's throat! Be careful what you do with wooden knives. Battered and chipped ends can become splinters.

# Chapter 4

# Knife Fighting Grips

### Grip 1: The Saber Grip

A popular way to hold a knife is blade-out, commonly called the "saber" grip which points the blade tip outward toward the target. Then there are more specific sub-categories or versions of the saber grip, one is an attacking "Filipino" grip, the second, a vice-like "blocking or anti-disarm" grip and the third version, the "forefinger/scalpel" grip. Finally, there is a little known, less-used "two finger beside the blade" grip.

Each grip offers advantages and disadvantages. The consummate knife fighter should know them all and should train to shift hand grippings for the appropriate action.

*See photos on next page*

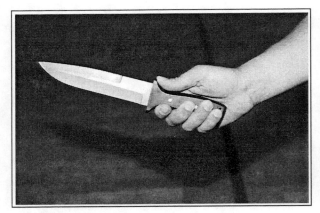

FIlipino saber grip

Saber blocking and anti-disarm

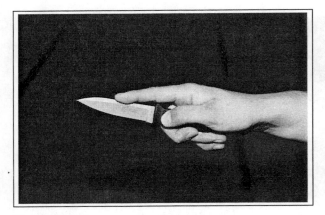

Scalpel grip

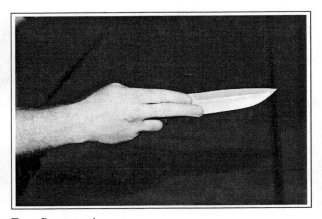

Two-finger grip

## 1) The saber Filipino grip

The "Arnis" or Filipino grip is a wise way to saber grip a knife through the majority of a fight. In the Filipino grip, one holds the blade handle lower in the fingers, curling the fingers around the grip and leaving the upper palm mostly free. The thumb is usually positioned atop the knife. This grip is anatomically, "user-friendly" to the wrist, increasing the range of motion for stabbing and slashing. Then you can always resort to the death grip if strategically needed. It frees the wrist for adequate blade twisting, and you must remember it is important to twist the blade upon, or after a stab. This opens the wound canal and frees the blade for a withdrawal against the suction and density of the body.

Part of this Filipino grip is the optional use of the thumb on the top of, or just over, the top of the knife. The thumb can act as an instinctive directional pointer to the target, and can be lifted up an inch or two from the knife top and used for limited trapping of the enemy, hooking wrists, hands, arms, clothing, whatever, as part of your attack.

If you choose to use this "thumb-wise" grip the majority of the time, you must carefully select a knife with a comfortable hilt, no top guard (you can severely jam or injure your thumb against one) and a blade whose back top edge is flat just off the handle, around your thumb's working area. Be careful! As you will find in the knife disarm drills in the upcoming chapter, the opponent's access to your thumb helps him disarm you!

## 2) Saber "blocking" or anti-disarm grip

A novice knife fighter will pick up a knife in this sword-like saber grip and place the handle high into the palm of the hand, in a tight, vice-like, "death" grip. The forearm muscles will ripple. This vice grip severely limits the range of motion of the wrist and therefore stabbing and slashing ability. A complete death grip on the knife handle tightens the hand and fingers, thus tightening the muscles of the forearm and then subconsciously, maybe even the biceps. Tightness slows a fighter down, slows stabbing and striking down. Looseness facilitates speed. There are times for this high and tight grip, for example at the precise second you feel a disarm of your knife is imminent.

A death grip on the blade might quickly counter the disarm. Also, if you use the knife as a blocking tool vs. a handstrike, kick, or weapon, you had better "knuckle-down" to withstand the impact,

then shift to a more aggressive grip. To prevent disarms, wrap the thumb around the handle to grip. To block, you might use the thumb up the backstrap of the knife to support the blade against impact.

## 3) The saber scalpel grip

This grip is used by surgeons and should be used by the knife fighter when such precision work is required. It brings alive your all-purpose and instinctively-trained index finger. The index finger runs up the backstrap of the blade and controls the motions of the attack. If you think you cannot get more control of a knife with this grip, try writing some words on a piece of paper without the use of your index finger on your pen!

## 4) The saber two-fingers-beside-the-blade grip

This is a grip I was shown in the Philippine Islands by a knife expert as an important one in his repertoire. He liked it for blade control and straight-line stabbing. But to me, the pommel is not supported sufficiently in the heel or thumb muscle of the palm. After all, two fingers beside the flat of the blade leaves only two fingers to clutch the grip!

I believe this grip originated from the curved handles often found on Southeast Asian, South Pacific, and Spanish knives. This curved handle fits more snuggly in the palm of the hand, when these two fingers are up beside the blade. In the real world of modern, straight-handle stabbing, this grip is not solid enough to routinely succeed.

## Grip 2: The Reverse, Concealed or "Icepick" Grip

The blade of the knife protrudes out of the bottom of the hand in this grip. It is called the reverse grip because it is the opposite of the standard and popular Saber grip, and therefore is in reverse position. That is why the reverse grip is often called the "icepick" grip, because the knife can be used in that commonly identified, icepick-stabbing fashion.

Front and side photos of reverse grip in fighting stance

The reverse grip can be used for:

a) slashing

b) stabbing

Sometimes, at the user's discretion, the thumb is placed on top of the pommel, or handle's end, for downward stabbing power and control.

without thumb stab

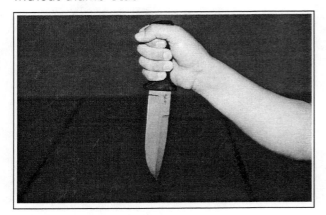

with thumb stab

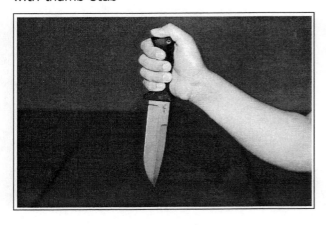

horizontal stab photo

vertical stab

c) limited trapping

Trapping or immobilization of the opponent's limbs can be conducted in this grip, by pinching the limb between the blade and the forearm.

d) blocking

e) The concealed grip:

It is sometimes called the "concealed" grip because, if practiced (in a mirror) properly, a fighter can learn to hide the blade from an opponent by placing it up against his or her forearm. Then fire it into attack or defense action.

## Grip 3: Switching Grips and Hands Drills

Now that I have established these differing saber and reverse grips, I need to emphasize the need to not only be able to switch knife grips back and forth in the same hand, but also to switch hands during a fight for attack and counter-attack strategies. These tricky and risky techniques can be practiced through the famous Filipino attribute developing drill called "Hubod," detailed in later chapters of this encyclopedia.

a) Switching from saber grip to icepick grip:

A skilled knife fighter spends training time with his favorite knife in his hand, working the blade from saber to icepick grips and back again. The specific circumstance of the fight will dictate which grip is the smarter. For example, you may always practice drawing your blade from your pocket and have it always snap out into the saber position. But you might need to pull it sometime and hide it in the concealed grip casual stance to take an approaching opponent by surprise.

After your first icepick, concealed assault, you might need to switch back to the longer range saber grip. Take care to select your knife. I have seen knives with brass-knuckle style handles and enclosed individual finger guards, or sub-hilts. These handles and guards will restrict or inhibit your grip-switching capability and therefore limit your knife fighting potential.

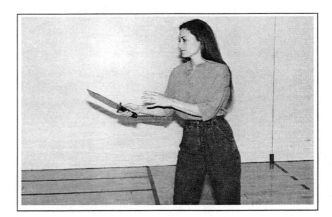

b) Switching hands to counter disarms: When one thinks of switching knife hands, one conjures up an image of the choreographed dance/fight scenes in "West Side Story," where young punks switch hands before an opponent. This is not the kind of technique I advocate. There are specific and strategic times to switch your knife hands. During a knife fight, the opponent may attempt a push/pull style knife disarm. Usually, the opponent will clutch and pull your weapon-bearing thumb and/or hand, and with his blade or the back of his other hand, will push on your blade. If you feel your knife coming free, snatch it with your own free hand rather than let it fly free from the push/pull inertia.

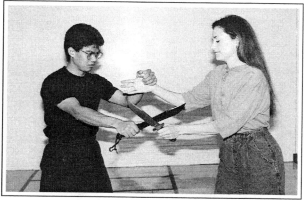

c) Switching hands to counter trapping: The opponent may also trap and/or pin your knife-carrying arm. This is a good time to switch your knife hands to counter these attempts.

e) Switching hands to continue fighting after injury:
If your weapon-bearing limb is injured, to survive the battle you must be able to switch off to the uninjured hand.

f) Knife-edge turning:
Sometimes your knife-edge is down, and it might need to be edge-up to maximize your attack. The knife fighter will have to rotate the knife in his or her hand to put the edge in the best position.

Changing grips is not new to the martial arts. For example, there are some Japanese Tanto knifes curved in such a way that some martial artists instruct turning the knives upside down in the hand so a thrusting stab can have maximum success. In the same vein, there are katana (samurai sword) schools that turn their blade upside down during a thrust to maximize a stab, or turn the edge of their sword away from another sword's impact when possible, to block an incoming sharp edge attack.

d) Switching hands to hit a surprise target:
If your knife hand is fully engaged in a medium to close-quarter encounter, sometimes it is strategic to quickly switch hands and attack an unprotected target from the other side. A hand switch may open a new target that your original knife hand didn't have. Remember, switching hands is dangerous in the chaos of a fight, but it might be your best option to attack.

## Grip 4: Practice Drills

Here are some training progressions you can practice from a fighting stance:

1) Multiple grip pass-off
   a) Saber Filipino grip to,
   b) Blocking and anti-disarm grip to,
   c) Reverse grip to,
   d) Switch hands to,
   e) Reverse grip to
   f) Blocking and anti-disarm grip to,
   g) Saber Filipino grip to,
   h) Switch hands...

2) Saber Filipino grip pass-off from one hand to the other
3) Reverse grip pass-off from one hand to the other
4) Saber Filipino grip pass-off from one hand to the other in a reverse grip
5) You construct any grip-changing, hand-changing combination...

Series of fan switch

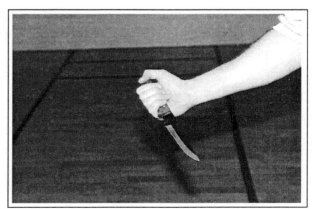

Series of finger switch

1

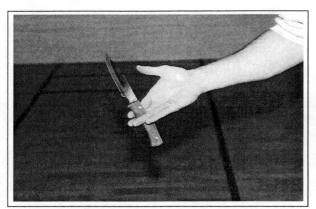

3

2

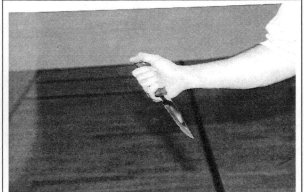

4

# WARNING

### The Thumb-High Cancer Grip

There is a cancer growing in knife instruction. Famous and influential instructors, and their thoughtless imitators are perpetrating a dangerous cancer-the thumb high grip. In this grip, the holder's thumb is about an inch above the knife, and the handle of the knife is low in the fingers of the hand. This grip appears in famous videos and even on the cover of another knife book!

The thenar-or the ball of the thumb-and the thumb itself, can be responsible for 45 percent to 65 percent of a grip on a knife. Take this Cancer Grip and slash and stab a heavy bag. Try dressing out a deer. The knife will tumble out of your hand. Use it in a real knife fight, and it will become a deadly mistake. It might look very, very pretty, and therein lies its infectious success. Pretty.

A thumb-high grip has very limited practical use in hooking or trapping, but there still exists the strong risk of having the knife dislodged from your hand. Some suggest that the high thumb has some kind of pointing or targeting advantage. If that is the case, why not bring the thumb down on the blade in the practical Filipino Grip, more in line with the knife tip? The high thumb just looks pretty, that is all. In real life combat, it is a Cancer.

## Summary

There are two basic grips, the saber and reverse grips and some variations with each.

No one grip is universal for all encounters, or universal for all tasks in any one encounter. Therefore, grip-switching is an important skill requiring your development and study. Practice switching grips. Do not select a fighting knife with features like brass knuckle grips, enclosed finger guards or, sub-hilts (extra small hilts down the handle, or anything exotic that will obstruct a quick grip switch! If you must make such a selection, you must practice to overcome the impediment.

I prefer two basic saber grip styles. For attacking, I and a great many other knife fighting experts like the lower-in-the-hand Filipino grip with the maximum use of the thumb atop the blade for control, guidance and limited trapping. This is also good for counters to blocking and disarming, a quick switch to the vice-like tension of the "blocking and anti-disarm" grip.

Practice switching hands to:

a) counter certain disarms
b) counter trapping
c) make a surprise attack on an unprotected target
d) continue fighting after a weapon-bearing limb injury

Here are some training progressions you can practice from a fighting stance:

a) Multiple grip pass-off drill
   1) Saber Filipino grip to,
   2) Blocking and anti-disarm grip to,
   3) Reverse grip to,
   4) Switch hands to,
   5) Reverse grip to,
   6) Blocking and anti-disarm grip to,
   7) Saber Filipino grip to,
   8) Switch hands...

b) Saber Filipino grip pass-off from one hand to the other
c) Reverse grip pass-off from one hand to the other
d) You construct any combination...

# Chapter 5

## Knife-Carrying and Drawing

### Consideration 1: Carry Sites on the Body

Where you will carry, and how you will draw your knife will depend greatly on three factors, the size, weight and type of the knife. Will it be a folding knife or an "unfolding" fixed blade. Comfort and concealment are important. You must also decide if you want to cross draw the knife from a carry site on your weak side to your strong side hand. Or do you want to carry and pull your knife all on your strong side? Below are some carry sites and related quick-draw considerations.

**Carry site consideration 1: The print**

Are you concerned with visibility and concealment? In police work, there is a term we use called a "print." This means there is a print, or the outline of the surface of a weapon pressed against someone's clothing. It could be the outline of a handgun's grip pushing out against a coat jacket. This is also true with knives. Do you care that your knife leaves a detectable print against your clothing? Do you care that your folding knife displays its handle clip on the outside of your pocket for all to see you have a knife?

**Carry site consideration 2: "Rookie" movement**

Even if you have successfully hidden your blade, will your naive physical actions give it away? A rookie policeman or detective carrying a concealed handgun often pats the weapon regularly, especially when sitting down, or standing up from sitting, such as in a restaurant or getting in and out of a car. These are two times to observe behavior for concealed weaponry. These are movements you must avoid, or look for in a potential opponent.

**Carry site and quick-draw consideration 3: Pocket carry**

Inside a pants pocket is a good place for a folding or lock-blade knife, and maybe even for an appropriate sized fixed blade with some pocket-toughening modifications.

a)  Pocket-clip carry:
    Many lock-blade and folding knives now have clips on their handles, so you may clip the closed folder to your pocket edge. With some practice, you will always know where your blade is and how best to quickly open the blade. I have seen some solid, or one-piece-fixed blades with handle clips for belts, pantlines or pockets, but you need a tough pocket and maybe even a steel thigh!

b)  Loose or deep pocket carry:
    Many people just carry their folding knives loose in their pockets. This may slow quick-drawing time down because first you have to bury a searching hand into your pocket and seek out a good grip. Depending upon your unfolding

mechanism, this loose pocket carry can then cause unfolding problems. What is your method of opening this blade? Is it a thumb hole in the blade? A small thumb-catch? In loose-pocket carry, you must first find the blade in your pocket, then find by finger sensitivity-the unfolding mechanism. The knife might be upside down from a quick-draw position. You cannot predict whether the blade will come out in a saber or reverse, icepick grip.

c)  Sheath pocket carry:
    The size of your knife or the pocket may allow you to slip a blade-sheath and all-into the pocket, but you had better devise a way to secure the sheath inside the pocket so that the blade can be pulled from the sheath and pocket, simultaneously. Otherwise the knife and sheath will be drawn out together, causing quick-draw problems.

    There is a Filipino strategy that involves throwing the sheath of a knife at an attacker as a distraction, and while that might be a problem-solving option, you don't want to slow your quick-draw down.

**Carry-site and quick-draw consideration 4: Beltline carry**

There are many methods and directions one can beltline carry.

a) sheath outside the belt and vertical,
   1) cross draw side or,
   2) strong side.
b) sheath concealed inside the pants and vertical,
   1) cross draw or,
   2) strong side.
c) sheath outside the belt and diagonal,
   1) cross draw or,
   2) strong side.
d) sheath concealed inside the belt and diagonal,
   1) cross draw or,
   2) strong side.
e) sheath inside the belt loops—horizontal —usually in the small of the back area, or anywhere there is a flat enough surface to comfortably carry a horizontal knife.
f) knife hidden inside a belt buckle.

## Carry-site and quick-draw consideration 5: Shoulder holster

Some knives are carried in a shoulder harness such as a handgun in a shoulder holster. Usually the blade handle is:

1) down or,
2) slanted slightly to the front, to clear the sheath and body during a draw or,
3) down, up, or slanted and cleared by a Velcro style break-away sheath.

## Carry-site and quick-draw consideration 6: Boot carry

Some knives are carried inside the boot by way of a clip on the knife handle, or a clip on the knife sheath. These are difficult to get to, fast, if you are wearing long pants. First, you have to clear your pant leg from the boot high enough to get to, and then draw, the knife.

## Carry-site and quick-draw consideration 7: Ankle sheath

Some knives are strapped to the carrier's ankle in a holster, similar to a handgun style carry, hidden under the long pant leg or trousers. Like the boot draw, difficult to get to fast.

## Carry-site and quick-draw consideration 8: Forearm holster

Some small knives are strapped to the inside of a carrier's forearm, hidden under a long sleeve of a shirt. The more the handle is concealed, the slower its accessibility and quickdraw.

## Carry-site and quick-draw consideration 9: Thigh sheath

Some carry an exposed knife in a sheath about thigh high and about arm or hand's length. This is for maximum quick draw.

**Carry-site and quick-draw consideration 10: Clothing sheath**

Some sew a sheath into their clothing, such as to the inside of their jackets, shirts, etc. The more concealed, the slower the quickdraw.

**Carry-site and quick-draw consideration 11: Necklace sheath**

Wearing a knife in a decorative sheath, handle-down like a necklace, lets the wearer hang the blade onto his chest or hang down the backbone.

**Carry-site and quick-draw consideration 12: Body anatomy**

I have been involved in several police cases where handguns and drugs have been concealed in the anus, or taped into the armpit, or in the crotch area. Where a gun or a bag can go, a knife can travel. This is more of a problem for law enforcement in customs and incarceration situations.

**Carry-site and quick-draw consideration 13: Carry items**

Knives can be carried, or concealed in attache cases, store bags, laptop computers, canes, backpacks, anything that someone might carry on their person, yet is not securely attached. A slight diversion can produce a quick-draw.

# Consideration 2: Drawing the Blade

**Draw consideration 1: Same-side draw or cross draw**

Do you wish to carry and draw your knife on the same side of your body? In other words, your knife might be clipped to the right side of your pocket, and you wish to draw it with your right hand. This is a "same-side" draw. Or do you wish to cross-draw your knife, meaning for example that your knife is carried on the left side of your body and drawn with your right hand? You would have to "cross" your body to pull the weapon.

**Draw consideration 2: Cover strategies**

Either way, same-side draw or cross-draw, an educated opponent can detect these motions as threats if the moves are not cleverly covered by a physical distraction or verbal excuses. Some example covers are:

a) Verbal covers:
   1) Stall by offering money for your life and act like you are reaching for a wallet. Pull your knife.
   2) Yell for help. Pull your knife.
   3) Point off to the side announcing the presence of help or witnesses. Pull your knife.

b) Physical covers:
1) Wave your hands in a nervous fit. Pull your knife.
2) Pull your wallet and flip it toward the opponent. Pull your knife.
3) Turn your body in a nervous fit, concealing your draw.
4) Pretend to throw up, or grow faint from the encounter, then pull your knife.
5) Push the opponent away from you, then pull your knife.
6) Strike the opponent, then pull your knife.
7) Dodge, fake, cut, or back-peddle and draw during or after this evasive footwork.

I could not possibly list all the clever and impromptu ways to cover your pull. They could be as singular as faking vomiting, or passing out. It will depend upon the situation, where on your body you carry your knife, and how much distraction time you need. For example, if you boot-carry a folding knife, you will need to raise your pant leg, clear the folded knife from your boot, then open it!

You will need a substantial distraction to accomplish this.

## Drawing consideration 3: Drawing into the proper grip

Carrying your knife upside down in a shoulder holster will reward you an easy saber grip. Select a practical quick draw grip from your carry site.

## Drawing consideration 4: Drill the quick draw

Whatever type of knife you select, or wherever you choose to wear it, practice an economical and practical draw and slash, stab or block. Due to the variety of carry sites and knives, I can only offer these most generic pointers:

a) Practice seeking and gripping the handle of the knife.
b) Practice drawing the knife from its carry site. Remember to experiment by utilizing your body to facilitate the pull. For example, if your knife is on your hip, lower your hip as you pull the blade. This helps clear the knife from the sheath that much quicker.
c) If it's a folder, practice opening it a multitude of times and ways. Keep your folder lubricated.

Some knives can be opened partially by hand, and then let the gravity of a whip-like slash open it the rest of the way.

One way to do this is to draw up the knife and extract the blade about 85 percent. Then, at an angle toward your target, snap the knife at the target as you start your attack. This economical snap should completely open the folder just before hitting the target. This shaves about

15 percent off the blade opening and attack process.

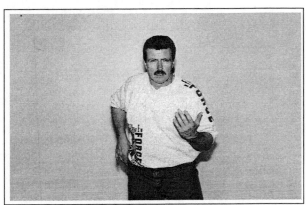

d) Buying time to quickdraw in close-quarters.

For the sake of training, let us presume that your knife is clipped in your pocket, or belted to your side for a quickdraw.

Here are some quickdraw strategies and dangers against an armed protagonist:

1) Push the opponent's torso, and maneuver away while drawing. The danger with this is, you may get your pushing limb cut.

2) Low-line kick the opponent to the knees or shins, maneuver away while

drawing. The danger with this is, if the kick is not fast enough, debilitating enough, or low enough, he could get you.

3) Grabbing the weapon-bearing limb and striking the face, then maneuvering to draw. The danger being he might cut you. You might miss the grab, and he might cut your incoming strike.

4) Get away while drawing the knife.

The same quick-draw strategies pertain to a confrontation with an unarmed aggressor, however the dangers are lessened. He may only grab your intentions, not cut them into a bleeding wound.

e) Get into your balanced knife fighting stance during or instantly after the draw.

**Draw consideration 5: Stealth draw of the locking blade knife**

What if you are hidden in an alleyway and an attacker is approaching. You need the element of surprise, and extracting your lockblade knife and snapping it open involves a metallic clicking sound as the blade locks back into position. This telltale sound would alert the enemy. You should practice opening the knife and with a finger, keeping the release mechanism depressed. Cushion the seating so the blade can seat quietly. You have a stealth draw!

# Chapter 6

# Knife Fighting Stances and Strategies

### Strategy 1: Four Fundamental Knife Fighting Stances

A fighting stance is where a fight begins, like a runner waiting in the starting blocks gets into his or her best position to start a race. A stance should not be mistaken as a statue position. There are four basic knife fighting stances, strong-side/hand forward stance, strong side/hand back stance, the casual or concealed grip stance, and finally the unarmed vs. the armed.

### Fundamental stance approach 1:

Strong-side forward, that is when the most coordinated hand holds the knife, and the strong side shoulder and leg are forward. This puts the knife up front in the fight. The strong-side forward is favored by many experts in knife vs. knife encounters, for its optimum range reach. This too is my common sense choice. I favor this strong-side forward stance in a knife vs. knife encounter.

Strong-side forward

Strong-side back

## Fundamental stance approach 2:

Strong-side back, that is when the most coordinated hand holds the knife back, and the empty hand side, shoulder and leg are forward. This puts the knife back from the fight. The strong-side back is favored by many experts when you are the only one armed in an encounter. These experts profess that with a strong-side back stance, you are "protecting" the knife against disarms, and your free hand forward can help establish your attack with trapping, striking or faking the opponent to set up your knife attack. I sometimes favor this

when you are armed and the opponent is not.

Few theory fighters prefer holding their strong-side back in a knife vs. knife en-counter, but I don't believe these theorists have even knife-sparred to see that putting your unprotected forearm up front before an armed opponent can get it sliced to ribbons. Also, your lunge ability is limited in this strong-side back position, because as in a cross punch, your knife hand has to cross the distance of your body first, then close the distance between you and the opponent.

Strong-side back places your up-front arm as a target in a knife fight

1

4

2

5

3

Twice the distance to attack with your strong-side back

### 3) Fundamental stance approach 3:

The causal, or concealed grip stance, where the person stands in a balanced, yet casual and unassuming stance. The knife is carried in the "icepick" or reverse position, and is hidden by the forearm from the opponent's vision. This stance is supposed to surprise the enemy when you spring into the attack.

### 4) Fundamental stance approach 4:

The unarmed defensive stance: We have explored many different knife fighting stances and must discuss a stance for the unarmed person facing a knife-attack. The same concepts of balance in motion are in play. Mobility is the key. Evading the

blade is paramount. When there is no hope for escape, and you cannot use items in your environment to protect you, turn the back of your forearms outward to the armed opponent. Minimize the damage. This puts the delicate forearm muscles and the inside of your wrists away from the knife. Using the basic unarmed blocks and possible disarms listed later in this work, do the best you can. Don't forget your low-line kicks and hand strikes.

## Strategy 2: Two Strong-Side Forward Basic Fighting Stances

In theory, a fighting stance is really about balance in motion, and the chaos of a fight will carry a fighter into many awkward positions and predicaments. When out of balance, regroup. Return to your favorite fighting stance as a base. Try to keep your hips under your shoulders.

There are only two common sense approaches to a knife fighter's combat stance, and the knife fighter should fluctuate between a fencer's approach, and a kickboxer's approach, during an encounter:

a)  Fencers narrow themselves as a body target by turning their body sideways from the opponent. This also accentuates lunging footwork. But remember, fencing rules have physical boundaries. Their "arena" is essentially a rectangle, forcing the players to move mostly forward and backward.

b)  Kickboxers do offer a 45-degree body target by quarter-turning away from the opponent. But this allows them to use both their legs/feet and arms/hands as in-range weapons and allows them greater side-by-side mobility.

When in the kickboxing phase, your knife fighting stance should resemble that of a boxer—light, mobile, fast—with both forward, backward and side-to-side mobility. NO WIDE-LEGGED CLASSICAL MARTIAL ARTS STANCES.

Remember that knife fighting requires mobility and speed. Try to imagine how Mohammad Ali or Sugar Ray Leonard might move in a knife fight. In this stance, you should be on the balls of your feet most of the time for mobility. There is a modern adage, "The balls of your feet are the gas petal, the heels are the brakes." This of course does not preclude dropping down on your heels for a power base or balance. Some classical martial arts systems are obsessed with being flat-footed, but for mobility that should not always be the case.

Your feet can be shoulder-width apart with the rear foot about 45-degrees back from the front foot. This brings the torso around and allows the rear hand quicker access and engagement into the fight. This also creates a stance for efficient kicking.

## Strategy 3: The Window of Combat

### a) Knife hand in the window

Whether you are fighting in the strong side forward stance, or strong side back, keep the knife hand in motion in a window of combat. This imaginary window is a rectangle loosely bordered by your shoulders and hips. Rearing the blade back well beyond these boundaries gives your opponent more time to react and block. As a rule, try to point the tip of the blade at the opponent as if it were a flashlight shining on him.

The modern martial arts concept of economy of motion dictates simplicity and efficiency of movement. The economic attack works on the most direct path from weapon to target. Often, in my martial arts travels, I see what I call "pretty Arnis or pretty Kali," here in the United States, where a practitioner routinely over-does his slash, taking the attack well beyond the window boundaries. Never over-slash unless it is part of your strategy.

Keeping the knife in motion in the window of combat turns it into a moving target and makes the knife hand elusive and harder to grab, slash or disarm. Motion also makes the knife hard to track when you use it to attack. The opponent never knows from what "quadrant" of the window you are about to fire an attack. These same principles of motion and attack hold true with your backup hand.

**b) Backup hand in the window**
The backup hand can serve many purposes. Just its motions, either mimicking the blade or maneuvering in the opposite direction of the blade, can distract and even somewhat hypnotize the opponent. Then it fires out to strike, push or pull the opponent in the encounter.

If the opponent is armed with a knife, our back hand needs to remain as safe as possible and avoid the opponent's attack.

As detailed in previous chapters and photos, it is good practice to turn the backup hand palm-inward, when it is not in immediate use. This turns the major blood vessels on the wrist away from the opponent's knife.

Your backup, empty hand needs to remain in this window for follow-up action. Do not "glue" this backup palm to your chest. This hand-glued-to-the-chest looks real pretty. Pretty Kali. Many practice this to a fault. I have even seen one American/Filipino system that routinely encourages students to place their backup hand completely behind them, palm up, as if they were serving a pie on a plate to someone directly behind them! It looks very pretty!

This type of abuse of the backup hand is as bad as the mindless practice of positioning your fist on your hip, so often seen in classical movements. Thousands of these repetitions carve a negative path of muscle memory. I have seen hundreds of students try to make the transition from the classical arts to more modern, scientific systems, and have a reflex of re-cocking their fist on their hip between major and minor body movements. And what else should we expect? Classical martial artists do thousands of these repetitions in their career.

Then when these classical students put on the gear to spar, their instructors must wean them away from these impractical hand postures. "Oh, oh get your fist off your hip!" "Keep your hands up!" The first time a student is told this (myself included 25 years ago) we all want to say, "Why then did you teach me the other way?"

That is of course, if the instructors have enough sense to correct them. It is almost unbelievable to say that some instructors don't. I have been in several tournaments through the years where I have seen some very exotic and esoteric Asian systems compete. One such system encourages students to always place one hand behind them while the other hand punched forward. Looks real balanced and pretty, much like this "pie-serving" technique except it was done with a fist and not a palm-up, open hand movement. When they got on the mat to fight modern groups, such as Kempo and other systems, all of which fought more like Thai boxers, the esoterics were all slaughtered like lambs. Slaughtered!

I remember in Tulsa, Oklahoma one time, I saw such an esoteric group destroyed match after match, up until the last man. This final contestant threw out four years of his martial art study, and kept both his hands in the window of combat just to save his head and survive. Untrained in this modern stance, and shaken to his core, he too lost quickly. Perhaps worse, was the shock of this group, this tournament obviously the first road test of their system. They felt as if their time training

was all wasted. Their spirit was destroyed. Impractical systems are a philosophical disgrace to the warrior spirit of which martial arts are supposed to exemplify.

Too much "glue-hand," "pie-serving," and "hip-cocking" practice repetitions will teach your muscle memory to fight...THE WRONG, UNECONOMICAL, UNSAFE WAY! THINK ABOUT IT!

**c) Window of combat shadow boxing**
Every technique and drill should be an exercise in study for the window of combat. But for your stance practice, here are some suggestions. Strike a fighting stance and move your knife hand and backup hand so that your:

1) knife hand moves side-to-side, backup hand moves in opposite or different motions,
2) knife hand moves up and down, backup hand moves in opposite or different motion,
3) knife hand moves diagonally, backup hand moves in opposite or different motion,
4) knife hand moves in figure 8 circular patterns, backup hand moves in opposite or different motion,
5) knife hand moves forward and back and backup hand moves in opposite or different motions,
6) "all the above"—confuse the opponent and set a razor shield in front of you.

7) using the 12 angles of attack drill, or any of the attack drill patterns in this encyclopedia. After each attack angle, interject your backup hand forward in some type of attack, like a push, or punch. Then with a partner before you, working the same angles, interject backup hand contact with your partner on the half-beats between the knife slashes.

These drills are demonstrated in Hock's knife fighting video series.

## Strategy 4: Which Hand Holds the Knife

My boxing coach once told me, "I fight with my strong side back, like all boxers. I save this for the fourth round!" And he raised a right-handed fist in the air. Of course he was referring to his power cross, the big knock-out punch, from his strong and most coordinated hand. Ever the student of street fighting tactics, I immediately asked myself, "Why wait for the fourth round?

To me, that is like saying, "I am going into a gunfight. I am going to use this pistol first for awhile, then pull out this machine gun later!" There is no fourth round in a gunfight, street fight, or a knife fight. The more you prolong an encounter, the greater your chances are that you will be injured or killed. Street fighting and knife fighting have no referee. Your strongest, most coordinated hand should hold the knife, whether you choose a strong-side forward, or strong-side back stance. Your object is to finish the fight as quickly as possible.

Most knife fighters will always have a strong hand preference. And this strong hand forward will position this same side leg and shoulder forward, dictating the foundation for your fighting stance. Elite empty hand fighters, after years and years of work, can completely loose a sense of strong side/weak side. But knife fighters pack knives somewhere on their body, and have knife-drawing considerations, and therefore must have a preference.

I am also a private student of Professor Remy Presas, and he declares, "I learn both left and right from the study of stick fighting." Filipino stick training, the "doble baston" and stick and knife study, the "Espada Y Daga," develops coordination to such a high point one can gain ambidextrous skills. You can also train in "doble daga," or working with two knives. I urge everyone to develop your so-called "weak-side" into mastery by working all drills and techniques with both hands.

Chapter 7

# Knife Fighting Footwork

## Strategy 1: Basic Footwork

In a fight, your footwork carries you through the four ranges of attack, the kicking range, the striking range, the trapping range (where arm and leg immobilization and manipulation occur) then the grappling range. Remember that a fighting stance is all about balance in motion brought about by footwork, and the chaos of a fight will carry you into many awkward positions and

predicaments. When out of balance, regroup. Return to your favorite fighting stance as a base.

In this chapter, you will find a list and brief explanation of some basic, universal, martial arts footwork. Once you master the footwork, then put a knife in your strong hand and slash, hack or stab as you move. Next, put a knife in your weak hand and do the same. Then use two knives and do this work. Keep flowing!

### 1) Stationary right foot—left foot steps forward and back

This is an excellent advance and retreat step that keeps you in range. From a fighting stance, leave your right foot stationary and step forward and back with your left foot.

### 2) Stationary left foot—right foot steps forward and back

This is an excellent advance and retreat footwork that keeps you in close range. Do this from a stationary left foot, with the right stepping forward and back. This is advance and retreat footwork.

### 3) Shuffle footwork (the pendulum)

If you are shuffling forward, let your rear foot come forward near your front foot, and displace it, then let your front foot shift forward. They do not have to hit together, or your rear foot does not have to "knock" the front one forward. But this is sometimes a wise practice for the beginner to get the concept. The reverse is used for going backward. This is an exceptionally good move to increase the gap between you and your opponent in a retreat and to advance. It is also excellent for delivering many of the low-line kicks conducive to knife fighting.

### 4) Lunge footwork

Like a fencer, slightly lift your lead foot and propel yourself forward off of your rear foot. Do the reverse for going backward. Lift your rear foot, and spring back.

### 5) Lateral footwork

From the fighting stance, if you choose to go step to the right, then let your right foot step right. Let your left foot follow, and get back into a stance. If you choose to go to the left, then let your left foot first step to the left, then let your right foot follow. Then return to the stance. Try not to cross your feet, for this is a point of imbalance.

### 6) Triangle footwork

Imagine there is a "V" shape on the floor before you, or an upside down "V" before you:

a)  In the right side up "V," imagine there is an opponent in the open space of the "V." With a 45-degree step to the left, or 45-degree step to the right, you are advancing and zoning to either one side or the other of the opponent. These can be shuffle or lunge steps. There are many variations, follow-up steps off of this basic pattern, which will subtly be covered in later study.

b) In the upside down "V," you are retreating backward and then stepping forward to and from an opponent, with 45-degree steps to the right or left. These can be shuffle or lunge steps. There are many variation follow-ups also from this drill.

## 7) Boxing's rocker shuffle

From a fighting stance, slightly bounce your lead and rear feet in toward your opponent a few inches, then bounce both back again, shuffling back and forth, or side-to-side. Then change leads in motion and do so from there. Don't over exaggerate the bounce. Stay close to the ground.

## 8) Backpeddling

It is important to be able to back quickly away from a dangerous situation. In the gym, learn how not to trip over your own two feet. In the real world, you must be careful not to trip.

# Strategy 2: Footwork Drills

Here are some footwork drills.

## 1) The Presas 12 angle knife footwork drills

In the Philippines, weaponry is wisely taught first. In the case of footwork, you learn quick and crisp footwork by stepping away from a knife or a stick. There is an immediacy about evading a swinging and stabbing weapon that enhances your ability.

In order to maximize this, we must first put to memory the famous and comprehensive Presas family Arnis angles of slash and stab attack. These 12 angles are important to memorize because they will appear again in different parts of this encyclopedia as attack drills and skill-developing drills. The 12 angles are:

1) Forty-five degree downward slash to the left side of the opponent's neck area.
2) Forty-five degree downward slash to the right side of the opponent's neck area.
3) Horizontal shoulder/upper arm high slash to the left side of the opponent.
4) Horizontal shoulder/upper arm high slash to the right side of the opponent.
5) Straight line stab anywhere to the opponent's midsection.
6) High straight line stab, knuckles inward, to the opponent's heart.

7) High straight line stab, knuckles outward to the opponent's right breast.
8) Low 45-degree slash to the opponent's right thigh.
9) Low 45-degree slash to the opponent's left thigh.
10) Straight stab, knuckles inward, to the opponent's left eye.
11) Straight stab, knuckles outward, to the opponent's right eye.
12) A downward slash.

Now, have one practitioner stand as a trainer before a trainee. The armed trainer will run through these angles of attack, and the unarmed trainee must avoid the attack by:

a) lunge footwork vs. the 12,
b) shuffle footwork vs. the 12,
c) side-stepping to the right or left vs. the 12,
d) stationary right foot and left step,
e) stationary left foot and right step.

These 12 angles of diverse attack, offer knife fighters a way to comprehensively familiarize themselves with all the types and angles of attack in one drill and train footwork against them.

After each evasion, the trainee must return back in range, exercising the same footwork to practice the next move.

For example, here is the breakdown for shuffle footwork practice:

a) The trainer slashes angle 1:
The trainee shuffles back to avoid the blade,
The trainee shuffles forward before the trainer to continue with angle 2.
b) The trainer slashes angle 2:
The trainee shuffles back to avoid the blade,
The trainer shuffles forward before the trainer to continue with angle 3.

## 2) Circle drill with partner

With a trainer before you to set the direction and pace, let him maneuver around you. You never let the gap between you change, and you always try to stay in an appropriate range and stance before him. In other words, if he is at the 12 o'clock position, you be at the 6 o'clock position.

## 3) Sprint drills

Sprint drills are good warm-up drills, that need sufficient space. Use safe speeds. These are straight line dashes.

a) one dashes into the attack against a distant and stationary partner.
b) one dashes while a partner back-peddles for retreat.
c) one dashes to a trainer and knife-attacks a focus mitt.

d) one dashes and traps a trainer's limb to clear a path for a knife attack.

e) one dashes up to and does knife Hubod with a retreating partner. The Hubod drill is detailed in later chapters.

f) one dashes up to and does a give and take, Sumbrada drill. The Sumbrada drill is detailed in later chapters.

## 4) Chase drill with partner

Good after warming and understanding the sprint drills. There are three versions of this chase drill:

a) being chased:
Keeping your balance and as much of a working stance as possible, let a training partner chase you in all directions in what might be as realistic a fight as possible. This will help you keep your balance and bearings. Remember to slowly develop speed during this drill.

b) chasing:
Keeping a working balance, pursue an evading training partner.
Remember to slowly develop speed during this drill.

c) a freestyle mix of both:
Mix up the two preceding drills.
Remember to develop speed slowly during this drill.

## 5) Knife sparring with partner

See Chapter 18 for the details. Not only are these very combat savvy, but knife sparring offers some of the best footwork development on earth!

## 6) Solo/aerobic drills

The following are an excellent series of knife and footwork drills to develop wind, muscle and coordination.

The basic directions are:
1) straight forward
2) forward and 45-degrees to the right
3) forward and 45-degrees to the left
4) to the right
5) to the left
6) straight back
7) backward and 45-degrees to the right
8) backward and 45-degrees to the left

The four basic stances to work these footwork drills originate from:

1) right-handed and strong-side forward
   a) saber grip, b) reverse grip,
2) left-handed and strong-side forward
   a) saber grip, b) reverse grip
3) right-handed and strong-side back
   a) saber grip, b) reverse grip
4) left-handed and strong-side back
   a) saber grip b) reverse grip

Once you have established the basic directions of travel and the stances and grips, select footwork techniques and practice. For example:

**Drill example breakdown: The lunge and saber grip stab**

1) Select a stance
2) Select a saber or reverse grip
3) Work lunge and stab repetitions through the 8 directions. Spend time in each direction such as 10 reps for each direction.
4) Switch hands

Here are just a few of the many drill combinations:

1) Inward slash and lunge
2) Backhand slash and lunge
3) Reverse grip stab and lunge
4) Saber stab and shuffle
5) and so on...

These drills are great, aerobic ways to warm up a knife fighting class or have a solo workout.

# Chapter 8

# Knife Target Strategies

### Target Strategy 1: The Impact of Wounds on the Sane and Insane

Did you know that more than half the edged-weapon murders in this country are committed by mentally deranged people? Do mentally deranged people respond like normal people?

There are many martial artists I respect and admire who preach a hard line on the immediate and irrefutable success of a single knife slash upon the enemy. If I might paraphrase some of these statements...

*"One cut, and the shock will incapacitate the opponent."*

*"A single cut, anywhere on the body will wipe a guy's concentration out."*

*"There will be immediate fear and shock. He will pass out in a minute."*

*"One cut, even on the forearm..and it's all over!"*

You get the idea. Strong words. Now, far be it from me to say that the knife doesn't cause incredible and lethal injury, or that the horror of being cut or stabbed isn't significant. But you will never hear a REAL veteran soldier or, in most cases, an experienced police officer take these statements for granted—nor should you as a streetfighter. For, you see, we have seen crazy people. We have seen adrenalized people. We have seen drugged people. Sometimes nerves get severed in a cut, and the victim is pain free. Like Duracell batteries, some "just keep on a going!"

As a police officer, I have seen people attack their families, friends and police, and then hope they themselves die in the process! More than once I have heard, "Go ahead and kill me! You may as well kill me right now!" Time and time again, these lunatics, drugged or not, can overlook their knife and gunshot wounds and keep on attacking.

What happened to all those "shocked, fainted, and babbling" knife victims all these martial arts instructors preached to me about?

You cannot count on the fact that a victim of a knife attack will curl up in the fetal position before you!

So you see, I truly believe there are smarter places to stab and cut rather than other reasons for these strategies. These strategies involve three categories:

1) Time delay tactics,
2) Immobilization and disabling tactics,
3) Kill tactics.

All of the following target strategies in this chapter concern themselves with these topics.

## Target Strategy 2: Delay Wounds

Delay wounds might be best defined as an injury that takes a few seconds or more for total impact. It is a delayed reaction.

### Delay wound A: The forehead cut

Obtaining a significant slash across the brow, or the forehead of an opponent should bring by gravity, a blood flow down upon the eyebrows and into the eyes.

Anyone who has experienced sweat flowing into their eyes could imagine what it might be like to have your own blood, thicker than sweat, in the eyes. While it might not be your primary target during a knife fight, realize the value of getting a forehead cut on the enemy. If you stall through footwork and sparring skills, your next entry could be more successful against this semi-blinded or distracted opponent.

### Delay wound B: Defanging the Snake

Defanging the Snake is a term usually attributed to the Filipino Martial Arts. A snake without its poisonous fangs cannot hurt you. It refers to a strategy that focuses an attack directly on the weapon-bearing hand of the opponent. Don't waste precious time slinging your blade wildly in the air and miss an opportunity to cut the opponent's weapon hand or limb.

## Delay wound C: Eye attacks

David slew Goliath with a rock to one of his giant eyes. A superficial eye wound can blind or partially blind the opponent into either watery or bloody eyes. Partial or total darkness for your opponent increases your chances of success. The eye cavity is a soft canal to the brain for stabbing, and more than a superficial wound can be deadly.

## Delay wound D: The vital bloodline attacks

Arteries and veins carry blood to and from parts of the body. Cutting or stabbing a main artery is a lethal problem for the victim. Basically, significant cutting and/or stabbing in or on the neck, in or on the clavicle, inside the biceps, inside the wrist and the thigh, are major bleeding targets.

But simply remember, while there are major bleeding targets, anywhere you penetrate the skin, there will be blood. Some of these wounds can cause death in 10 seconds! The opening of a bleeding wound can cause significant physiological and psychological shock. Blood rushes to the wound and leaves other vital areas, such as the brain with a lack of pressure that can induce weakness and fainting.

If you inflict such a major wound on an opponent, you might spring back and observe for a second if possible, to see if he registers these reactions. Then move in for the finish if need be, or just stand back safely for 10 or more seconds.

## Target Strategy 3: Immobilization Wounds

Immobilizing wounds can be defined as those injuries that should, to some significant level, paralyze a part or perhaps all of the opponent's body.

### Immobilization wound A: Backbone attacks

Severing the discs, and attacking the nervous system on the spinal cord is a disabling and debilitating act, especially if you target the back of the neck/base of the skull area. Often, this is an easily accessible area, naked and visible as opposed to clothed and padded. Remember, as in the rib cage attacks, turn your blade sideways for easier entry.

### Immobilization wound B: Arm muscle attacks

A slice severing the arm muscles or plucking the tendons of the arms can incapacitate the limb.

1) Deltoid cuts can inhibit the raising and turning of the arm.
2) Bicep cuts can inhibit the bending of the arms.
3) Tricep cuts can inhibit the bending of the arms.
4) Cuts across the forearms can inhibit the use of the fingers.

### Immobilization wound C: Leg muscle attacks

1) Upper leg cuts can be bloody and can inhibit the raising and lowering of the leg.
2) Cuts on the calf and shin can inhibit standing and foot manipulation.
3) Injury to the Achilles tendon can inhibit standing, walking and running.

### Immobilization wound D: Torso muscle attacks

1) Cutting the chest muscles can inhibit limb movement.
2) Cutting the back muscles can do the same.
3) Cutting lower torso muscles breaks the connection between the upper and lower body.

Another point can be made about torso muscle attacks. A major cut here can release internal pressures, and with the aid of gravity, expose the contained vitals, as shown in a photo in the introduction of this encyclopedia.

## Target Strategy 4: Killshots

### Killshot A: The ear canal and ear area

For centuries, military sword and knife instruction included topics about attacking the enemy on or about the ear.

"The ear canal is an open path to the brain. The canal path forgoes the thick skull," is a quote from a British commando manual. A thin double-edged commando style dagger is a perfect weapon for this penetration. Also, an easily and lethal penetration can be acquired right behind the ear lobe, a spot long considered a sensitive pressure point.

## Killshot B: The rib area stab

The rib cage protects the vital organs of the chest, the lungs and the heart. Getting a thrusting stab into these vital organs is a major coup for the knife fighter. In our terms, the rib cage becomes an obstacle in the way of our survival. There are many cases on file where the rib cage has halted a knife attack, or a rib has been chipped or broken, impeding the success of the attack. One main way to overcome the cage is to realize that ribs run horizontally. In order to achieve ultimate penetration, the blade should be turned horizontally to match.

## Saber grip acquisitions

1) When forced to attack on the opponent's centerline, or more to your left, his right, this can be achieved in the saber grip position by turning your grip palm-up and feeding it into the target area in this manner. (The reverse if you are left-handed.)

2) When forced to attack on the opponent's left side, your right, this can be

achieved in the saber grip by turning your grip knuckles up and feeding it into the target area in this manner. (The reverse if you are left-handed.)

## Reverse grip acquisitions

1) When forced to attack on the opponent's centerline, or more to your left, his right, this can be achieved in the reverse icepick grip by turning your grip knuckles up and feeding it into the target area in this manner. (The reverse if you are left-handed.)

2) When forced to attack on the opponent's centerline, or more to your left, his right, this can be achieved in the reverse icepick grip by turning your grip palm-up and feeding it into the target area in this manner. (The reverse if you are left-handed.)

## Killshot C: Under the chin attacks

One very soft, and incredibly painful, distracting, debilitating and killing spot to stab is under the chin. It affects major nerve centers and the throat.

## Killshot D: Neck attacks

The body assigns the neck to pass oxygen down through it and blood back up to the head. Then oxygen depleted blood travels back down into the torso. It is a soft conduit of energy to our computer—the brain. Cutting or stabbing the throat is a fast killer.

### Killshot E: Heart attacks

Significant stabs to the heart, by way of the chest, underarm and back are usually fatal.

Stabbing someone downward and deeply inside the left clavicle puts the blade into or near the upper part of the heart. Once this blade is in place, moving the handle severely side-to-side can rip the top of the heart.

## Target Strategy 5: Exiting Techniques

### Exit wound case study

I investigated a police case once when a knife-wielding suspect attacked another man in an apartment complex parking lot. Witnesses saw the confrontation and called the police. Trying for a higher target, the suspect failed and stabbed the man inadvertently in the thigh, which is always a dangerous wound. As the police sirens approached, the suspect tried to retrieve his knife. But, the victim's leg muscles and suction seized the knife and the blade. The suspect fled, abandoning the evidence of his attack. The knife had to be removed in the emergency room. Oddly enough, there was little blood loss because the knife itself acted as a band-aid!

### Exiting strategies

A novice might think that a simple stab or thrust into an enemy might be like popping a water balloon or tearing open a bag of jelly. Not always so! As discussed many times in this encyclopedia, a human, as well as an animal, is made up partly of gristle, muscle and bone. Sometimes your stab and slash can get hooked or stuck in the enemy, and not just in the body, but into and around clothing.

One way to get a feel for this realistic blade resistance is to go hunting and prepare large game for transport and eating. Another way might be to bury a knife into a tree to a point where it is difficult to retract the knife. This is something most everyone has done in a tree or in wood. How to retract the blade? You have to wiggle, twist and pry it out until a chip of the tree may fly free with the knife.

Twisting the blade upon entry, or in penetration can open the wound canal and assist the knife exit, but may not be the most efficient. Twisting the blade upon the exit stroke confronts problems with the immediate exit. This is the exiting strategy of which I speak. When you stab or thrust in practice, think about finishing the action with:

1) harsh yanking,
2) twisting and pulling,
3) prying, gaff-like motion.

## Backup hand assisted exits

Often I see expert knife fighters push the opponent away with their free hand to assist in the exiting of the blade from a torso wound. This is a fine strategy if the opponent in unarmed. I am sad to report however that there are knife experts touring the country and selling videos proposing that you use this technique...AGAINST ARMED SUBJECTS.

This is the safer way. Your backup hand can sometimes drop its guard duty and assist in the exit.

This strategy is crazy against an armed opponent! Crazy! Do you really want to take your guard hand away from covering that deadly blade to assist the exit? I don't think so! The opponent's unchecked knife hand could get you intentionally or accidentally wounded or killed.

## Chapter 9

# Saber Grip Knife Fighting Techniques

## Introduction

These exercises, techniques and drills constitute the fundamentals required for successful saber grip knife fighting. Training these techniques and corresponding foot work into muscle memory will create optimum ability and develop the "Flow." Mastery of the saber grip includes three separate studies, basic exercises and basic and advanced drills.

**1) Basic exercises:** These are the exercises that develop the slash, stab, hack and blocking techniques. They are designed to build speed, strength and coordination.

> Exercise set 1: Saber stabbing practice
> Exercise set 2: Hacking practice
> Exercise set 3: Slashing practice

**2) Basic drills:** These are the set patterns that explore and teach proper muscle memory. Without working the whole drill patterns, you will shortchange your muscle memory by not training the varying high and low angles. A summary of these major saber grip exercises and drills is given below.

> Drill 1: The 8 angle slashing drill
> Drill 2: The 8 angle double slash drill

Drill 3: The 8 angle slash and stab drill
Drill 4: The 10 angle stab and gaff drill
Drill 5: The 8 angle hacking drill
Drill 6: The Presas 12 angles of attack

## 3) Advanced drills: Counters to common blocks

Advanced practice "counters to common blocks" is a term and philosophy I learned from one of my greatest instructors and mentors, Professor Gary Dill. Professor Dill is always concerned with common sense street fighting and how to defeat the reflexive blocks of the opponent. In Jeet Kune Do, this is called "trapping hands." In Filipino Mano Mano, it's sometimes called "Tapi Tapi."

Practicing to defeat blocks carries the drill movements and flow one giant step closer to reality fighting.

All these drills are demonstrated in Hock's knife fighting videos.

## Exercise Set 1: Saber Quickfire Targeting

These are some basic saber grip stabbing exercises to get you familiar and proficient with stabbing at a target from the saber grip. The purpose is to translate these maneuvers into muscle memory. The actual drills introduced later in this chapter will advance you into the "Flow." Saber grip stabbing basics you should consider while you are performing these exercises are:

### 1) From high to high: High target stabs from high attack points

When your knife is going to attack from the upper portion of the window of combat, you should turn the blade somewhat to facilitate the stab. This will improve your attack by freeing up the joint capability of your wrist. The palm of your hand will turn upward, as though you are "serving up the knife," or your palm will turn outward, as though you are harpooning the knife.

If you stab from a right-handed grip and from above the solar plexus line to a target similar in height:

a)  stabbing from your high left, turn your hand palm upward.
b)  stabbing from your high center, turn your palm upward.
c)  stabbing from your high right, turn your palm downward or outward.

(If you stab from a left-handed grip and from above the solar plexus, just reverse the above.)

a) From your high left to the opponent's high right, turn your hand palm upward. Here, Billy Mills poses as my target.

b) From your high center to the opponent's high center, turn your palm upward.

c) From your high right, to your opponent's high left, turn your palm downward or angled outward.

## 2) From medium to low, medium or high: High stabs from medium or low attack points

You can keep the stabbing blade vertical or horizontal from a medium or lower start in the window or combat. These approaches work well with your wrist joint. You can also use the palm-up or palm-out stab.

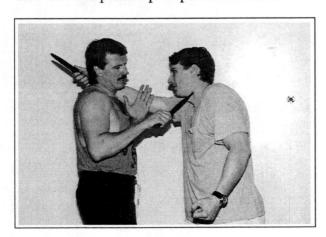

In this photo, I attack Tony Mobley from a lower start into the higher target of his neck. A completely horizontal blade with a palm-up or palm-down grip, would be very uncomfortable at this angle.

## 3) From low to low, medium and high:

At this range, when piercing into the lower waist, groin and lower targets, the wrist and arm functions the best with a vertical blade.

## Saber exercises

These described exercises will be done with a partner and a focus mitt. You will need two partners, a trainer or a trainee. The trainer will use a dot or mark on a focus mitt for the trainee's target acquisition. Remember to use a soft knife! Your focus mitts won't last long under a metal, wooden, or even a hard rubber blade. Work both right and left leads.

## Stationary exercise drill 1:

Hold the mitt as a still target and work repetitions of high, medium and low targets.

## Stationary exercise drill 2:

Flash the mitt to develop lunge and speed responses. Work repetitions of high, medium and low targets.

## Motion drill 1:

With a flashing mitt near different levels and areas, the trainer moves about before the trainee. This drill should maximize footwork. The trainer should reach out and attack the trainee on occasion just to keep the trainee "honest."

## The stab/lunge to the face

A stab straight to the face is an excellent attack technique to perfect. One of the hardest things to catch or hit in sports is a line drive, ground ball or tennis ball coming right at your centerline. Of course, the bigger the object, the easier it becomes to track, such as a football. Easier to see. Easier to focus. But, the tiny tip of a blade, flying at your centerline, is extremely hard to deal with, especially if:

a)  it is fired without telegraphing your intentions with setup body movements. For example, if you inadvertently twitch or chamber your shoulder before the attack, it could alert your opponent.

b)  you are in the proper range. There are differing range strategies. The further away you are, the less successful you may be because you offer the opponent more reaction time.

If you attack the face from a low point in very close range to the opponent, this creates interception difficulties for him. For many, their cheekbones and nose can actually impair their vision for this style of knife attack, or even eye jab.

c)  you don't try to strike with super force, just super speed!

This is not a jab "TKO" punch. This is a razor sharp attack to one of the most delicate and important body parts of the enemy. Accent the speed, not power. Remain loose and relaxed before, during and after firing the attack.

d)  you fire the stab from a constant motion in the window of combat. Keeping your knife hand still makes it easier for the opponent to surveil. If it is in motion, he will have a difficult time predicting from what quadrant of the window the knife will explode from.

You will have to practice this with a trainer who is wearing a helmet and a face shield to develop this particular skill. But practice this you must. This is one of the most powerful and effective techniques in this whole encyclopedia. If you are quick enough, you can use this successfully against armed opponents.

My students and I have "chinked" the face protection of armed opponents in knife sparring sessions before they could respond and caught their attack, either on the way in or on the way out.

## Exercise Set 2: Saber Grip Hacking

These are some basic exercises to get you familiar and proficient with hacking in the saber grip. Again, the purpose is to translate these maneuvers into muscle memory. The actual drills introduced later in this chapter will advance you into the "Flow." Saber grip hacking basics:

1) the blade hits with penetrating impact and retracts, like a axe chop. The bigger the knife, the better.

2) In the hack, you momentarily grip the knife severely to reenforce the impact. You may or may not use the thumb for impact support.

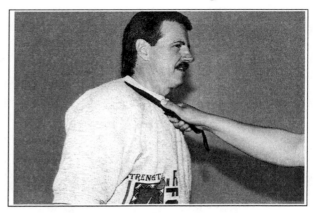

Hacking grip with a thumb support

3) There is a backhand hack that flies at the opponent like a backfist or a backhammer strike.

A backhanded strike: front and side view

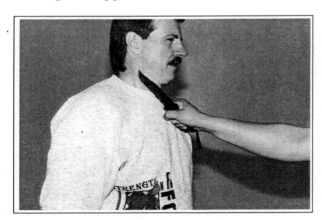

Hacking grip without a thumb support

4) Then there is an inward hack, from your "outside" to the opponent.

An inward strike: front and side view

Execute the following exercises from a mobile, "shadow-boxing" style fighting stance. You won't necessarily need a dot on a focus mitt as you might need for pinpoint stabbing. You need a surface like a focus mitt, Thai pad or a bag heavy enough to take the punishment. Again, use a soft knife to protect your training equipment.

**Stationary exercise drill 1:**

The trainer holds up a target, be it focus mitt or a Thai pad, and the trainee fires repetitions. Train for target acquisition and IMPACT! Work the left and right hand grip for:

a) series of high inward hacks
b) series of high backhand hacks
c) series of medium height inward hacks
d) series of medium height backhand hacks
e) series of low inward hacks
f) series of low backhand hacks
g) series of downward hacks
h) series of upward hacks

In this example series, Lloyd Fitzpatrick holds a stationary/fixed mitt for Elizabeth Fitzpatrick to attack.

## Stationary exercise drill 2:

Flash focus mitt at varied heights to develop speed.

In this example series, Lloyd feeds Elizabeth a flashing mitt. The faster he flashes, the faster she must strike.

## Motion exercise drill:

In a sparring environment, Lloyd moves about, flashing the mitt at differing levels and angles.

1

3

2

4

## Exercise Set 3: Saber Grip Slashing

These are some basic exercises to get you familiar and proficient with slashing in the saber grip. Again, the purpose is to translate these maneuvers into muscle memory. The actual drills introduced later in this chapter will advance you into the "Flow."

a) You strike across and through the target, raking or drawing the blade. Try to imagine an apple hanging from a string. Try to slash through the apple without the apple moving!

b) Once you have engaged the target, don't allow the blade to drop too far beyond the target. Keep the slashes economical.

**Stationary exercise drill 1:**
The trainer holds up a target, and the trainee fires repetitions. Train for slashing impact and target acquisition.

a) series of high inward slashes
b) series of high backhand slashes
c) series of medium inward slashes
d) series of medium height backhand slashes

e) series of low inward slashes
f) series of low backhand slashes
g) series of low downward slashes
h) series of upward slashes

**Stationary exercise drill 2:**
The trainer will flash the focus mitt for the above strikes.

**Motion exercise drill:**
The trainer will move about as if sparring, flashing one or two focus mitts.

Please refer to the two prior sections for the step-by-step photographic examples of how to proceed.

Do not over slash, sometimes ignorantly reinforced in classical training. It allows the opponent a window of opportunity to counter attack.

## Drill 1: Eight Angles of Saber Grip Slashing Knife Attack

When slashing, the blade should be "drawn through" the target, and these 8 angles of attack constitute an attribute-developing exercise to hone slashing skills, target acquisition, and the "Flow." They are more for the practitioner's slashing, flowing, muscle memory, than the target acquisition. For example, the opponent could turn sideways, in which case a practitioner's 8 angle delivery would be the same, only the target would be different.

### The figure 8 consideration

This drill consists of four figure 8 patterns.

When performed in succession, every two angles should create a "figure 8" configuration, flat figure 8 when slashing horizontally, and a vertical figure 8 when working angles number 7 and number 8. This consideration should help you memorize the drill. Three horizontal figure 8's, and one vertical figure 8.

Inside these four flowing figure 8 patterns are eight slashing knife attacks. Place the impact priority on the slash, and then loosely follow through in the figure 8 pattern to set up priority impact for the next slash. All slashes should be as economical as possible. There is no need to rear the blade back like a woodsman chopping with an axe.

### The backup hand

The backup hand remains in motion inside the window of combat, is all that is needed. One must use this free, hand for guard, trapping, follow-up strikes or body manipulation such as grabbing, pushing or pulling. Keep the free hand moving in the window of combat while you do these exercises. Do not drop it to your side or glue it to your chest.

### Develop both left and right

Work these first with the right hand, then the left. For left-handed flowing continuity, please reverse the sides. For example, in a left-handed attack, angle 1 would attack the right side of the opponent's body.

Here is a photographic series of the drill, from both a front and side view. Helping me are my students, Black Belt Elizabeth Fitzpatrick and Eric Grajo. Remember, these are still photographs of what is meant to be a flow.

Angle 1: Right-handed slash to the left side of the opponent's face or neck area.

Angle 4: Right-handed slash to the right side of the opponent's shoulder, bicep or rib area.

Angle 2: Right-handed slash to the right side of the opponent's face or neck area.

Angle 5: Right-handed slash to the left side of the opponent's thigh area.

Angle 3: Right-handed slash to the left side of the opponent's shoulder, bicep or rib area.

Angle 6: Left-handed slash to the right side of the opponent's thigh area.

Angle 7: Upward slash to the top areas of the opponent or under his chin. Think of first cutting the groin, slashing up the middle of the torso to the face.

Angle 8: Downward slash from the upper to the lower parts of the opponent's body. Think about cutting the top of the head, shoulders or the face, down to the middle of the torso.

Practice this drill:

a)  in the air,
b)  against a heavy bag to develop power,
c)  against a person to develop targeting skills.

## Counters against common blocks advanced drill practice

One angle at a time, attack a training partner, and allow him the time to throw up one or more defensive blocks. Depending upon the energy of the block, respond by:

1) **Trapping hand counters:** Push, pull or pin the block with your backup hand, and continue the attack. Work this through one block, then work a series where the trainer throws up a second block.

2) **Cutting counters:** When your knife attack is blocked, cut the blocking limb.

3) **Counter attack counter:** Your attempt thwarted? Immediately counter attack on a different angle.

This drill is demonstrated in Hock's knife fighting videos.

## Drill 2: Eight Angles of Saber Grip Multiple Slashing Knife Attack

As detailed in the previous drill, when slashing, the blade should be "drawn through" the target and these 8 angles of attack constitute an attribute-developing exercise to hone slashing skills, target acquisition, and the "Flow." They are more for the practitioner's slashing, flowing, muscle memory, than the target acquisition. For example, the opponent could turn sideways, in which case a practitioner's 8 angle delivery would be the same, only the target would be different.

### Double slashing

Start with the double slashing. When you slash down angle 1, you are palm up at a 45-degree angle. Quickly reverse the palm and slash back, traveling on the same line. This reversal is a double slash. For a triple slash, do this three times, and so on.

### The backup hand

The backup hand remaining in motion inside the "window of combat," is all that is needed. One must use this free hand for guarding, trapping, follow-up strikes or body manipulation such as grabbing, pushing or pulling. Keep the free hand moving in the window of combat while you do these exercises. Do not drop it to your side or glue it to your chest.

### Develop both left and right

Work these first with the right hand, then the left. For left-handed flowing continuity, please reverse the sides. For example, in a left-handed attack, angle 1 would attack the right side of the opponent's body.

Assisting me in this photo series are Elizabeth and Eric. Remember, these are still photos of what is meant to be a double slashing flow.

Angle 1: Right-handed slash to the left side of the opponent's face or neck area. Return slash one or more times.

Angle 2: Right-handed slash to the right side of the opponent's face or neck area. Return slash one or more times.

Angle 3: Right-handed slash to the left side of the opponent's shoulder, bicep or rib area. Return slash one or more times.

Angle 4: Right-handed slash to the right side of the opponent's shoulder, bicep or rib area. Return slash one or more times.

Angle 5: Right-handed slash to the left side of the opponent's thigh area. Return slash one or more times.

Angle 6: Left-handed slash to the right side of the opponent's thigh area. Return slash one or more times.

Angle 7: Upward slash to the top areas of the opponent or under his chin. Think of first cutting the groin, slashing up the middle of the torso to the face. Return slash one or more times.

Angle 8: Downward slash from the upper to the lower parts of the opponent's body. Think about cutting the top of the head, shoulders or the face, down to the middle of the torso. Return slash one or more times.

Practice this drill:

a) in the air,
b) against a heavy bag for developing impact power,
c) against a person to develop targeting skills.
d) work the "four corners."
   1) downward figure eights from the high right-hand position
   2) downward figure eights from the high left-hand position
   3) upward figure eights from the low right-hand position
   4) upward figure eights from the low left-hand position

The upward slashes are dynamic combat attacks!

## Counters against common blocks advance drill practice

One angle at a time, attack a training partner and let that partner throw up one or more defensive blocks. Depending upon the energy of the block, respond by:

1) **Trapping hand counters:** Push, pull or pin the block with your backup hand, and continue the attack. Work this through one block, then work a series where the trainer throws up a second block.
2) **Cutting counter:** When your knife attack is blocked, cut the blocking limb.
3) **Counter attack counter:** Your attempt thwarted? Immediately counter attack on a different angle.

This drill is demonstrated in Hock's knife fighting videos.

# Drill 3: Eight Angles of Saber Slashing and Stab Attack

This drill carries the fighter one step beyond the 8 angles of slashing into stabbing follow-ups. Using the figure 8 patterns and skills in the slashing drill and the stabbing, work this flowing combination. Working this slash and stab drill will actually improve your slashing because it will shorten your slash to execute a quick stab. You will place more emphasis on the impact of the slash, and you will shorten the follow-through to quicken the lapse between the slash and stab.

## The stabs

For the purpose of this drill, the high angle slashes require a high return stab to the throat. The low angle slashes require a stab to the groin.

## Develop both the right and left

Work these first with the right hand, then the left. For left-handed flowing continuity, please reverse the sides. For example, in a left-handed attack, angle 1 would attack the right side of the opponent's body.

Angle 1: Right-handed slash to the left side of the opponent's face or neck area. Stab to the throat.

Angle 2: Right-handed slash to the right side of the opponent's face or neck area. Stab to the throat.

Angle 3: Right-handed slash to the left side of the opponent's shoulder, bicep or rib area. Stab to the throat.

Angle 4: Right-handed slash to the right side of the opponent's shoulder, bicep or rib area. Stab to the throat.

Angle 5: Right-handed slash to the left side of the opponent's thigh area. Stab to the groin.

Angle 6: Left-handed slash to the right side of the opponent's thigh area. Stab to the groin.

Angle 7: Upward slash to the top areas of the opponent or under his chin. Think of first cutting the groin, slashing up the middle of the torso to the face. Stab to the throat.

Angle 8: Downward slash from the upper to the lower parts of the opponent's body. Think about cutting the top of the head, neck, shoulders or the face down to the middle of the torso. Stab to the groin.

Practice this drill:

a) in the air,

b) against a heavy bag for power development,

c) up against a person for target developing.

**Counters to common blocks advanced drill practice**

One angle at a time, have a training partner try to thwart your attack by throwing up one or more defensive blocks. Push or pull, depending upon the energy, respond by:

1) **Trapping hand counters:** Push, pull or pin the block with your backup hand and continue the attack. Work this through one block, then work a series where the trainer throws up a second block.

2) **Cutting counters:** When your knife attack is blocked, cut the blocking limb.

3) **Counter attack counter:** Your attempt thwarted? Immediately counter attack on a different angle.

This drill is demonstrated in Hock's knife fighting videos.

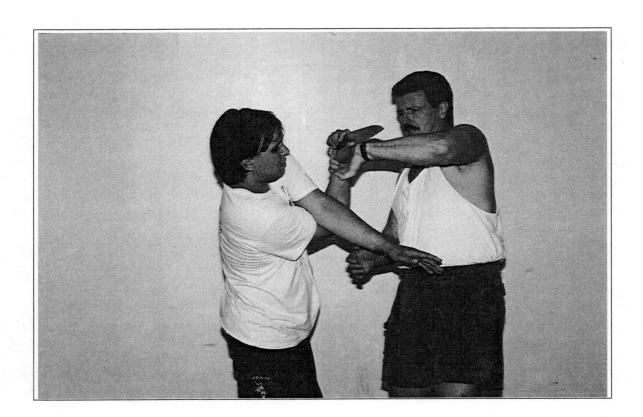

# Drill 4: Ten Angles of Saber Grip Stabbing Knife Attack

There are two basic stabs, a straight in stab or a hooking style "gaff" stab. The gaff can create a penetrating rip. This 10 angle drill works both. It will familiarize you with the major angles of attack.

## Straight stab

The straight stab is self-explanatory. Its components are made up from the saber grip exercises that appear earlier in this chapter.

## The gaff

The weapon or tool called a gaff is usually a pole with a sharp hook on the end, and this symbolizes our gaffing style attack. The tip penetrates in a stabbing motion and rips out in the curve of the gaff. The side-angle hooking style attack accentuates the flow of a gaff assault.

## The backup hand

The backup hand remains in motion inside the window of combat. One must use the free hand for guard, trapping, follow-up strikes or body manipulation such as grabbing, pushing or pulling. Keep the free hand moving in the window of combat while you do these exercises. Do not drop it to your side or glue it to your chest.

## Develop both left and right

Work these first with the right hand. Then the left. For left-handed flowing continuity, please reverse the sides. For example, in a left-handed attack, angle 1 would attack the right side of the opponent's body.

Angle 1: Hooking, palm-down stab to the left side of the opponent's face or neck area.

Angle 2: Hooking, palm-up stab to the right side of the opponent's face or neck area.

Angle 3: Hooking, palm-down stab to the left side of the opponent's shoulder, bicep or rib area.

Angle 6: Hooking palm-up stab to the right side of the opponent's thigh area.

Angle 4: Hooking, palm-up stab to the right side of the opponent's shoulder, bicep or rib area.

Angle 7: Upward stab to the top areas of the opponent or under his chin.

Angle 5: Hooking palm-down stab to the left side of the opponent's thigh area.

Angle 8: Downward stab from the upper to the lower parts of the opponent's body.

Angle 9: Palm-up stab to the opponent's chest.

Angle 10: Stab to the opponent's lower torso.

Practice this drill:

a) in the air,
b) against a heavy bag for power development,
c) against a person for target development.

**Counters to common blocks advanced drill practice**

One angle at a time, attack a training partner, and allow the partner to throw up one or more defensive blocks. Depending upon the energy of the block, respond by:

1) **Trapping hand counters:** Push, pull or pin the block with your backup hand, and continue the attack. Work this through one block. Then work a series where the trainer throws up a second block.

2) **Cutting counters:** When your knife attack is blocked, cut the blocking limb.

3) **Counter attack counters:** Your attempt thwarted? Immediately counter attack on a different angle.

This drill is demonstrated in Hock's knife fighting videos.

## Drill 5: Ten Angles of Saber Grip Stabbing and Slashing Knife Attack

As in the prior drill, there are two basic stabs, a straight in stab, or a hooking style "gaff" stab. The gaff can create a penetrating rip. This 10 angle drill works both. It will familiarize you with the major angles of attack.

### Straight stab

The straight stab is self-explanatory. Its components are made up from the saber grip exercises that appear earlier in this chapter.

### The gaff

The weapon or tool called a gaff is usually a pole with a sharp hook on the end, and this symbolizes our gaffing style attack. The tip penetrates in a stabbing motion and rips out in the curve of the gaff. The side-angle hooking style attack accentuates the flow of a gaff assault.

### The slash

Once the tip of the knife has entered the target, you make a sharp twist, which should position the sharp edge toward the enemy. Then slash the opponent. This "chips" open the original stab wound and is an excellent double attack method.

### The backup hand

The backup hand remains in motion inside the window of combat. One must use the free hand for guard, trapping, follow-up strikes or body manipulation such as grabbing, pushing or pulling. Keep the free hand moving in the window of combat while you do these exercises. Do not drop it to your side or glue it to your chest.

### Develop both left and right

Work these first with the right hand, then the left. For left-handed flowing continuity, please reverse the sides. For example, in a left-handed attack, angle 1 would attack the right side of the opponent's body.

**Angle 1:** Hooking, palm-down stab to the left side of the opponent's face or neck area. Twist the blade and slash.

**Angle 2:** Hooking, palm-up stab to the right side of the opponent's face or neck area. Twist the blade and slash.

**Angle 3:** Hooking, palm-down stab to the left side of the opponent's shoulder, bicep or rib area. Twist the blade and slash.

**Angle 4:** Hooking, palm-up stab to the right side of the opponent's shoulder, bicep or rib area. Twist the blade and slash.

**Angle 5:** Hooking palm-down stab to the left side of the opponent's thigh area. Twist the blade and slash.

**Angle 6:** Hooking palm-up stab to the right side of the opponent's thigh area. Twist the blade and slash.

**Angle 7:** Upward stab to the top areas of the opponent or under his chin. Twist the blade and slash.

**Angle 8:** Downward stab from the upper to the lower parts of the opponent's body. Twist the blade and slash.

**Angle 9:** Palm-up stab to the opponent's chest. Twist the blade and slash.

**Angle 10:** Stab to the opponent's lower torso. Twist the blade and slash.

Practice this drill:

a) in the air,
b) against a heavy bag for power development,
c) against a person for target development.

## "Counters to common blocks" advanced drill practice

You have already practiced these counters versus the first stabbing attack in a prior drill. This time, counter the slashing half of your attack. One angle at a time, attack a training partner, and allow the partner to throw up one or more defensive blocks. Depending upon the energy of the block, respond by:

a) Trapping hand counters: Pull, pull or pin the block with your backup hand, and continue the attack. Work this through one block, then work a series where the trainer throws up a second block.
b) Cutting counters: When your knife attack is blocked, cut the blocking limb.
c) Counter attack counters: Your attempt thwarted? Immediately counter attack on a different angle.

This drill is demonstrated in Hock's knife fighting videos.

## Drill 6: Eight Angles of Saber Grip Hacking Drill

These 8 angles of attack, constitute an attribute developing exercise to hone hacking skills, target acquisition, and the "Flow." They are more for the practitioner's hacking muscle memory, than the target acquisition of an opponent modeling before the practitioner. For example, the opponent could turn sideways, in which case a practitioner's delivery angle would remain the same, only the target would be different.

In all hacking, like almost all strikes in the martial arts, there can be hit and retract, or just a hit and an imbedding plant that remains for a second longer. Caution must be used in severe impact hacking. The blade could imbed deeply in the opponent. You might have difficulty pulling it free! The opponent could move or fall away with your weapon, and he could continue to fight for a period of time.

### Chambering the hack

As practiced in the hacking exercises, hacks should be as economical as possible. There is a need to rear the blade back like a woodsman chopping with an axe. Brief, too short and concise hacks may not get the desired effect, so one may have to rear back just beyond the usual boundaries of the window of combat. Again, the window of combat is the rectangle area before your torso in which the fight is engaged in.

### The backup hand

One must use the free, cover hand or "backup" hand for guard, trapping, follow-up strikes or body manipulation such as grabbing, pushing or pulling. Keep the free hand moving in the window of combat while you do these exercises. Do not drop it to your side or glue it to your chest.

### The grip factor

The grip is important when hacking. At the point of presumed impact, tighten your wrist and your hand like a vice on the grip to ensure solid impact. One may or may not, open and lift the thumb and brace it on the back of the blade for more support. The practitioner starts with the knife in the right hand.

### Develop both left and right

The following angles are from a right-handed grip. Work the drill with the left hand and reverse the angles. For example, a left-handed angle 1 hack would strike the right side of the opponent. This creates a better flow.

Angle 1: Hack to the left side of the opponent's face.

Angle 4: Hack to the right side of the opponent's shoulder, bicep/arm or rib area.

Angle 2: Hack to the right side of the opponent's face.

Angle 5: Hack to the left side of the opponent's thigh area.

Angle 3: Hack to the left side of the opponent's shoulder, bicep/arm or rib area.

Angle 6: Hack to the right side of the opponent's thigh area.

Angle 7: Upward hack into either the groin, or the chin or the torso if the body is bent over.

Angle 8: Downward hack to the head, face, shoulder or clavicle area.

Practice this drill:

a) in the air,
b) against a heavy bag to develop power,
c) against a person to develop targeting skills.

## Counters against common blocks advanced drill training

One angle at a time, attack a training partner, and allow him to throw up one or more defensive blocks. Depending upon that energy, respond by:

1) **Trapping hand counters:** Push, pull or pin the block with your backup hand, and continue the attack. Work this through one block, then work a series where the trainer throws up a second block.
2) **Cutting counters:** When your knife hand is blocked, cut the blocking limb.
3) **Counter attack counters:** Your attempt thwarted? Immediately counter attack on a different angle.

This drill is demonstrated in Hock's knife fighting videos.

## Drill 7: Presas Family 12 Angles of Attack

These 12 angles of attack are derived from Filipino Martial Arts, the Presas Arnis basic angles of attack. They constitute an attribute developing exercise to hone both slashing and stabbing skills, target acquisition, and the "Flow."

### Economy of motion

All striking actions should remain economical. Keep the knife hand in the window of combat. No retraction or chambering before slashing or stabbing. When slashing, the blade should be "drawn through" the target if possible.

### The blade twist

When stabbing, it is wise to twist the blade before, during or after the actual penetration to open the wound canal and ease knife withdrawal. Many times, human body muscular contraction and internal suction hold the knife in against withdrawal. A twist of the blade, not only does more damage, but inhibits these retaining body reactions.

### The backup hand

Like the other exercises and drills, one must use the free, cover hand or "backup" hand for guard, trapping, follow-up strikes or body manipulation such as grabbing, pushing or pulling. Keep the free hand moving in the window of combat while you do these exercises. Do not drop it to your side or glue it to your chest.

This drill is an excellent training skill-enhancing pattern. It must be memorized and can be fed to a training partner for a multitude of knife-fighting responses. This one drill includes both slashing and stabbing, therefore giving a partner an opportunity to respond to both major styles of attack. The Presas 12 angle drill will appear throughout this encyclopedia.

Angle 1: Right-handed slash to the left side of the opponent's face.

Angle 2: Right-handed slash to the right side of the opponent's face.

Angle 3: Right-handed slash to the left side of the opponent's shoulder, bicep or rib area.

Angle 6: Straight stab, knuckles inward, to the heart and chest.

Angle 4: Right-handed slash to the right side of the opponent's shoulder, bicep or rib area.

Angle 7: Straight stab, knuckles outward, to the right side of the opponent's chest.

Angle 5: Straight stab to the midsection.

Angle 8: Low back slash to the right side of the opponent's thigh.

Angle 9: Low slash to the left side of the opponent's thigh.

Angle 11: Straight high stab, knuckles outward to the opponent's right eye. You might grab the hair with your backup hand.

Angle 10: Straight high stab, knuckles inward, to the opponent's left eye. You might grab the hair with your backup hand.

Angle 12: A downward slash upon the side of the head or face, then a quick back stab under the chin.

Practice this drill:

a) in the air,

b) against a heavy bag to develop power,

c) against a person to develop targeting skills.

## Counters against common blocks advance drill practice

Since this versatile drill has both stabs and slashes, it is a thorough way to introduce even more study into harnessing the energy of the opponent's blocks. Try defeating a second block!

## The counter slash

Using the Presas 12 angles, have a trainer attack you with a knife. You respond with a slash to the weapon hand or wrist as in this series of photos.

Here, Elizabeth attacks Eric, and Eric counters with a slash.

1

3

2

4

### The grab and counter slash

Using the Presas 12 angles, have a trainer attack you with a knife. You respond with a slash to the weapon hand, a grab of the weapon hand to secure it and then another attack, be it a slash or a stab.

In this series of photos, Eric attacks Elizabeth with an angle 1, and she responds.

1

3

2

4

These drills are demonstrated in Hock's knife fighting videos.

## Chapter 10

# Reverse Grip Knife Fighting Techniques

## Introduction

These exercises and drills constitute the fundamental techniques required for successful reverse grip knife striking and footwork. Training these techniques with the corresponding foot movements will achieve optimum ability and also develop the "Flow."

The reverse grip allows a practitioner to conceal the blade for surprise attack or defense, by hiding it up against the forearm. Also covered are pommel strike exercises, commonly used to the reverse grip. The reverse grip can also offer limited trapping—the immobilization of the opponent's neck and limbs.

Basic Exercises

These exercises develop:
a) the reverse grip stab
b) the reverse grip slash
c) the pummel strike

Basic Drills

Drill 1: Eight angles reverse slashing drill
Drill 2: Eight angles reverse slash and stab drill
Drill 3: Concealed grip combat drill
Counters to common blocks: Advance practice drills

## Basic Exercises Set 1

### 1) Reverse grip stabbing exercise basics

These are some basic exercises to get you familiar and proficient with stabbing from the reverse grip. The purpose is to translate these maneuvers into muscle memory and develop targeting skills. The actual drills introduced later in this chapter will advance you into the "Flow."

When stabbing, whether vertical or horizontal, think of an icepick chipping into a block of ice. Reverse grip stabbing basics are:

a)  The blade can be horizontal or vertical.

b)  A stabbing reverse grip blade is usually 90-degrees from the forearm during the backhand stab.

c)  An optional technique is to place your thumb on the pommel upon impact.

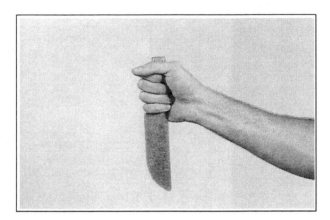

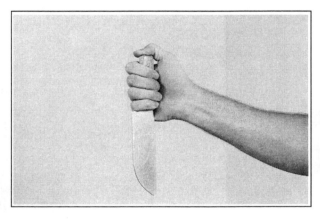

d)  Remember to try to twist the blade after penetration to open the wound canal for easier blade withdrawal.

e)  Execute these exercises from a mobile, "shadow-boxing" style fighting stance.

## Stabbing reverse grip exercises

The trainer holds a target before the trainee, such as a focus mitt or a heavy bag. Train from target acquisition and impact. Work right and left hands.

## Exercise 1: Stationary exercise series

The unmoving trainer holds the mitt for:

a) Series of high target stabs, mid-torso height targets, and groin or lower targets

## Exercise 2: Flashing mitts

Conduct these same attacks only with a flashing focus mitt.

1

4

2

5

3

## Exercise 3: Sparring motion

In sparring motion and with two flashing
focus mitts, work the trainee.

1

2

3

4

5

## Basic Exercises Set 2

### 1) Reverse grip slashing exercises

These are some basic exercises to get you familiar and proficient with slashing from the reverse grip. The purpose is to translate these maneuvers into muscle memory. The actual drills introduced later in this chapter will advance you into the "Flow."

a) Execute these exercises from a mobile, "shadow-boxing" style fighting stance.

### Slashing reverse grip exercises

The trainer holds a target before the trainee, such as a focus mitt or a heavy bag. Train from target acquisition and impact. Work right and left hands.

### Exercise 1: Stationary series

The unmoving trainer holds the mitt for:

a) Series of high, medium and low target slashes.

## Exercise 2: Flashing mitt

Conduct these same attacks only with a flashing focus mitt.

## Exercise 3: Sparring series

In sparring motion and with two flashing focus mitts, work the trainee.

## Basic Exercises Set 3

### Pommel striking exercise basics

Many martial arts systems ignore practice in pommel striking, while the military and some martial artists teach pommel striking techniques. My first introduction to knife fighting in the early '70s was at a Kenpo Karate school. We were taught to fight from a kickboxing stance, knife in reverse grip, incorporating a lot of pommel strikes.

A decade later, I trained with Retired Rhodesian Army Captain Ben Mangles, also a holder of six black belts. His emphasis on pommel striking brought to me a whole new appreciation of the technique.

Pommel striking can be executed from the saber and reverse grips. Pommel striking skills may be useful when:

a) you are rushed by an opponent and cannot bring your blade into action. Economy of motion might dictate a pommel strike to stun the opponent,
b) for whatever reason, you have decided not to use your blade to kill or maim this particular opponent.

These are some basic exercises to get you familiar and proficient with pommel striking from the reverse grip. I like to compare these pommel strikes to executing an empty handed ridge hand strike or hammer fists. The purpose is to translate these maneuvers into muscle memory.

Execute these exercises from a mobile, "shadow-boxing" style fighting stance.

Two basic delivery angles are:

1) straight line attacks,
    a) straight in,
    b) downward,
    c) upward.

2) any hooking angle attacks.

Some basic targets for the pommel strike are:

1) Face or throat

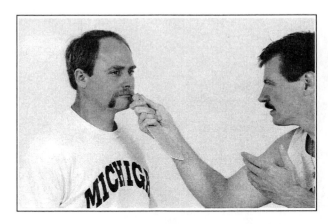

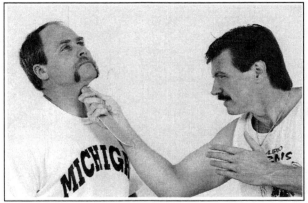

2) Side of the head

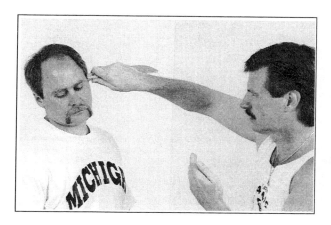

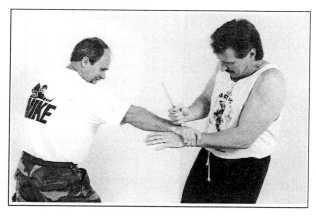

3) Groin

In this situation, a pommel strike is a wise choice. If you used the blade, you could stab yourself by accident.

4) Other

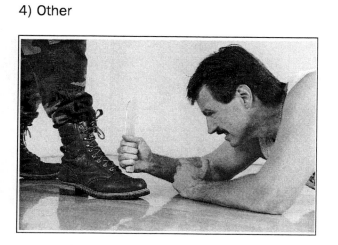

## Pommel exercises

The trainer holds a target before the trainee, such as a focus mitt or a heavy bag. Train from target acquisition and impact. Work right and left hands.

## Exercise 1: Stationary exercise series

The unmoving trainer holds the mitt for:

a) Series of high, medium and low target strikes:

## Exercise 2: Flashing mitts

Conduct these same attacks only with a flashing focus mitt.

## Exercise 3: Sparring motion

In sparring motion and with two flashing focus mitts, work the trainee.

# Drill 1: Eight Angles Reverse Grip Slashing Knife Attack

When slashing, the blade should be "drawn through" the target. These 8 angles of attack constitute an attribute-developing exercise to hone slashing skills, target acquisition, and the "flow." They are more for the practitioner's slashing, flowing, muscle memory, than the target acquisition. For example, the opponent could turn sideways, in which case a practitioner's 8 angle delivery would be the same, only the target would be different.

When performed in succession, these angles can create a "figure 8" configuration, a flat figure 8 when slashing horizontally, and a vertical, thin figure 8 when working angles number 7 and 8. Place the impact priority on the slash, and then loosely follow through in the figure 8 pattern to set up priority impact for the next slash. All slashes should be as economical as possible. There is no need to rear the blade back like a woodsman chopping with an axe.

The backup hand remaining in motion inside the window of combat is all that is needed. One must use this free hand for guard, trapping, follow-up strikes or body manipulation such as grabbing, pushing or pulling. Keep the free hand moving in the window of combat while you do these exercises. Do not drop it to your side or glue it to your chest.

Work these first with the right hand. Then the left. For left-handed flowing continuity, please reverse the sides. For example, in a left-handed attack, angle 1 would attack the right side of the opponent's body.

Angle 1: Right-handed slash to the left side of the opponent's face or neck area.

Angle 2: Right-handed slash to the right side of the opponent's face or neck area.

Angle 3: Right-handed slash to the left side of the opponent's shoulder, bicep or rib area.

Angle 4: Right-handed slash to the right side of the opponent's shoulder, bicep or rib area.

Angle 5: Right-handed slash to the left side of the opponent's thigh area.

Angle 6: Left-handed slash to the right side of the opponent's thigh area.

Angle 7: Upward slash to the top areas of the opponent or under his chin. Think of first cutting the groin, then slashing up the middle of the torso to the face.

Angle 8: Downward slash from the upper to the lower parts of the opponent's body. Think about cutting the top of the head, neck, shoulders or the face, down to the middle of the torso.

Practice this drill:

a) in the air,

b) against a heavy bag for slashing impact development,

c) up against a person for target development.

**Counters against common blocks advanced drill training**

One angle at a time, slash at an opponent. Let the opponent put a defensive hand/forearm up. Depending upon the energy, respond by:

a) **Trapping hand counters:** Push, pull, or pin the block with your backup hand, and continue the attack. Work this through one block, then work a series where the trainer throws up a second block.

**The "Pull" series.** If the blocking energy stops about halfway, grab it and pull it clear or pin the energy.

**The "Push" series.** Go with the blocking energy and pass the block, pushing it out of the way.

1

1

2

2

3

3

**b) Cutting counters:** When your knife hand is blocked, cut the blocking limb.

**c) Counter attack counters:** Your attempt thwarted? Immediately counter attack on a different angle.

## Drill 2: Eight Angles Reverse Grip Slashing and Stabbing Knife Attack

As detailed in the previous drill, when slashing, the blade should be "drawn through" the target. These 8 angles of attack constitute an attribute-developing exercise to hone slashing and stabbing skills, and the "Flow." They are more for the practitioner's slashing, flowing, muscle memory, than the target acquisition. For example, the opponent could turn sideways, in which case a practitioner's 8 angle delivery would be the same, only the target would be different.

When performed in succession, these angles can create a "figure 8" configuration, a flat figure 8 when slashing horizontally, and a vertical figure 8 when working angles 7 and 8. Place the impact priority on the slash, and then loosely follow through in the figure 8 pattern to set up priority impact for the next slash. All slashes should be as economical as possible. There is no need to rear the blade back like a woodsman chopping with an axe.

The backup hand remains in motion inside the window of combat. One must use this free, hand for guard, trapping, follow-up strikes or body manipulation such as grabbing, pushing or pulling. Keep the free hand moving in the window of combat while you do these exercises. Do not drop it to your side or glue it to your chest.

This time after each slash, you will return stroke with a stab.

Work these first with the right hand. Then the left. For left-handed flowing continuity, please reverse the sides. For example, in a left-handed attack, angle 1 would attack the right side of the opponent's body.

Angle 1: Right-handed slash to the left side of the opponent's face or neck area.

Angle 2: Right-handed slash to the right side of the opponent's face or neck area.

Angle 3: Right-handed slash to the left side of the opponent's shoulder, bicep or rib area.

Stab to the throat.

Stab to the throat.

Stab to the body.

Angle 4: Right-handed slash to the right side of the opponent's shoulder, bicep or rib area.

Angle 5: Right-handed slash to the left side of the opponent's thigh area.

Angle 6: Left-handed slash to the right side of the opponent's thigh area.

Stab to the body.

Stab.

Stab.

Angle 7: Upward slash to the top areas of the opponent or under his chin. Think of first cutting the groin, then slashing up the middle of the torso to the face.

Angle 8: Downward slash from the upper to the lower parts of the opponent's body. Think about cutting the top of the head, neck, shoulders or the face, down to the middle of the torso.

Stab downward into the clavicle.

Stab to the chin, torso or groin.

Practice this drill:

a) in the air,
b) against a heavy bag for impact power development,
c) up against a person for targeting skills.

## Counters against common blocks advanced drill practice

Attack a training partner, angle by angle. Let the trainer throw up a defensive block, on the stab. You have already worked the slashing portion on the previous drill. Depending upon the energy, respond with:

a) **Trapping hand counters:** Push, pull or pin the block with your backup hand, and continue the attack. Work this through one block, then work a series where the trainer throws up a second block.

b) **Cutting counters:** When your knife attack is blocked, attack the block.

c) **Counter attack counters:** Your attempt thwarted? Immediately counter attack on a different angle.

## Drill 3: The Alley Cat Street Fighter Progression Drill

The concealed grip drill is a reverse grip combat drill. The blade is hidden by your forearm from the view of an opponent in front of you. The edge must be facing out, that is to say that the edge is ready to slash out. The following is a six-count drill that will bring out the horror of this grip, as well as improve your coordination and speed.

The drill is a collection of some of the most deadly reverse grip techniques to be found. The concealed position has you in a comfortable stance with your hands at your sides, knife handle hidden in a hand and the blade hidden behind a forearm. As the blade fires from its concealed position to slash, the space between the blade and the forearm must increase to insure a flicking slash. These important pre-stab slashes can injure the opponent's torso or limbs, or cause a disarm if the opponent is armed.

When doing a realistic combat series, one can start in the concealed grip for the first angle attack, then execute any series of angles without returning to the concealed grip between each angle. Just go from slash and stab to slash and stab. In a realistic situation, there is no need to re-conceal the blade. The fight as already started in this training scenario.

To develop speed and flow, work the first two angles fast, then the remaining four regularly. Then train the first three rapid-fire, the last three slow. Then the first four fast, the last two slow. Work yourself up to all six.

Work this drill from both right and left-handed grips. Simply reverse the sides. For example, a left-handed angle 1 attack would be stabbing the right side of the opponent's body.

**Angle 1:** From the concealed position, the blade starts with a low upward diagonal cut-right to left, then turns direction mid-body, left to high right. The knife is then stabbed downward into the left side of the opponent's throat.

1

3

2

4

**Angle 2:** From the concealed position, the blade starts with an upper diagonal slash from low right to high left. The knife is then stabbed into the right side of the enemy's throat.

1

3

2

4

**Angle 3:** From the concealed position, the blade does a clockwise, half-circle at the mid-body, going left then turning right, so the blade stabs into the left side of the opponent's mid-torso.

1

3

2

4

**Angle 4:** From the concealed position, the blade slashes horizontally from right to left, then stabs into the right side of the opponent's body.

1

3

2

4

**Angle 5:** From the concealed position, the blade slashes straight up the body then plunges downward into head or face, upper part of the chest or clavicle areas.

1

3

2

4

**Angle 6:** From the concealed position, the blade does a low half-circle, counter-clockwise slash across the lower belly, then stabs the groin area.

Now lets put some reality into Tom's stance. You can see that following the pattern now proposes to attack the limbs, then the primary target.

Practice this drill:

a) in the air,
b) against a heavy bag to develop power,
c) against a person to develop targeting skills.

There is no official "counters against common blocks" drill associated with this concealed grip study. The circular delivery pattern before the stab is meant to disable any flak encountered along the way. Also, inherent in the drill itself is the backup hands involvement in clearing a path. Between the two, they should defeat the common blocks.

There are multiple realistic combat scenarios that can be developed from these patterns, as required by the Congress rank testing. There is a Congress video "Knife Street Fighter" Progression Drills that teach many of these scenarios. Practice being confronted by one or more opponents and counter with any of these patterns.

# Chapter 11

# Knife Blocking

## Blocking Strategy 1: Pros and Cons

There are respected knife fighting experts who believe that one should practice knife blocking techniques because blocks can be successful. Then there are respected experts who declare the opposite, that blocking a sharped-edged weapon attack, is both "ludicrous and suicidal." These negative experts state that a quick withdrawal and twist of the attacker's blade can easily counter your block as well as any disarm.

Now, I will ask you to become the expert. An expert in your own life and death. You are about to be attacked by a knife-wielding manic. There is no escape. You may be armed or unarmed, but you will most surely die, if you don't do something. You will never see your loved ones again, or your loved ones are standing behind you, sure to be the next victims after you. Would you like to go into this encounter with some blocking and disarming skills, or not?

The nay-sayers who claim all knife blockers are suicidal, aren't considering the fact that many, if not most, of all knife attackers are unskilled and ignorant fighters, who probably don't know about these twisting and withdrawing counters to blocks and disarms. And even if they do, if you are skilled enough through practice, you have a fighting chance! I want you to have at least a fighting chance! That is why I will not listen to the nay-sayers.

You have to do something to fight back, to minimize the wounding and counter attack.

If you are armed with a knife and using it to block an incoming knife attack, let your blade do the talking for you. You can do two things:

1) block the attack, and simultaneously cut the weapon-bearing arm,
2) at least block the knife with your knife.

A consummate knife fighter knows ways to use a blade, or empty hands, to block a knife attack. This chapter will explore using your knife in a saber or reverse grip to block incoming angles of attack. Study and drill. Save your life! Block and know how to block! Go down fighting! You may never have to go!

BUILD PROPER BLOCKING MUSCLE MEMORY!

All these blocking techniques and drills are demonstrated in Hock's knife fighting videos.

## Blocking Strategy 2: The Difference Between Aggression and Defensive Blocks

Remember the basic difference between an attack motion and a block motion.

1) An attack is an act of aggression.
2) A block is an instinctive and reflexive act of protection, which may or may not injure the opponent. A block is a response.

To stop an incoming force with the blade of your knife, you need a tightened grip on the handle. Some experts call it a hammer grip, some a vice-grip. There are five major ways for a knife fighter to block aggression:

a) blocks with a saber grip
b) blocks with a reverse or icepick grip
c) empty hand or backup hand blocking
d) forearm blocking
e) other tools

Reverse grip block

Hand blocking

Forearm blocking

Saber grip knife block

Other "tool" blocking

### Knife blocking

If you are blocking an attack with your knife, try to injure also on first contact. So, a knife block, by virtue of its sharp edge, can actually serve as a counter attack. If you block in a straight line, your block is like a hack. If you block and move the blade upon impact, you produce a slash. So, in many ways, these blocks resemble the slashing and hacking drills previously studied.

### Empty hand blocking

If your free hand/limb is blocking, perhaps at times the impact can be disabling, such as when your forearm bone strikes the weapon-bearing arm in a muscle or nerve area.

### Grip tension

Another major difference between slashing and blocking, is the tension of the grip upon the knife. When attacking, the lower-in-the-hand Filipino style grip can facilitate attacking. But, when using the knife to block the momentum of any attack, the instant of force to force contact, the high-in-the-palm "vice grip" should be implemented to counter the incoming force.

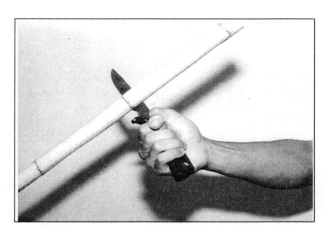

## Drill 1: Six Angles, Saber Grip, Basic Knife Blocking Drill

Let the cold steel of the blade do the blocking work. These are basic blocks with the saber grip. Each knife block could be used against any type of attack, such as an empty hand push, eye jab, punch, kick, etc., or a weapon attack. The best block is a cut! And this is a cut on first contact. It might lead to a quick disarm. The backup hand should follow the knife block in some attack if possible. Take note that these are hacking and/or pushing style blocks.

a) Hack blocks are like punches into the attacks, that may or may not push the incoming limb away.
b) Slash blocks are just that, with the intention to stop the force of the attack first, then draw through the target. The following series of six blocks completes one drill. Economy of motion will dictate whether a hack or a slice can be used.

This drill is detailed from a right-handed grip. Work it with the left hand also. Just reverse the angles.

1) Blade edge crosses your body from the right to the left side, to hack/block an opponent's right attack. The blade could hit any part of the attacker. It could strike the weapon, or the limb. Your body zones to the right.
2) Blade edge turns out to your right side and the left side of the opponent, to hack/block an opponent's left attack. Remember to accentuate the turning out of the hand, accentuating the knuckles. Your body zones to the left.
3) Blade edge crosses your body from the right to the lower left side in a sweep to block the opponent's lower right side attack. Your blade tip should be pointed downward. Your body zones to the right.
4) Blade edge turns out to your lower right side, to the lower left of the opponent's attack side, in a sweep hack/block vs. a lower left side attack. Your body zones to the left.
5) Blade edge high, Filipino "Crossada-style," in a upward hack/block vs. an overhead attack. The blade should intercept any downward attack and the backup hand pushes it off to the side.
6) Downward block, covering the centerline of the body.

1

2

3

4

5

6

## Drill 2: Six Angles, Reverse Grip, Basic Knife Blocking Drill

Let the cold steel of the blade do the blocking work. These are basic blocks with the reverse grip. Each knife block could be used against any type of attack, such as an empty hand push, eye jab, punch, kick, etc., or a weapon attack. The best block is a cut. And this is a cut on first contact. It might lead to a quick disarm. The backup hand should follow the knife block in some attack, if possible. Take note that these are hacking and/or pushing style blocks.

a) Hack blocks are like punches into the attacks, that may or may not push the incoming limb away.

b) Slash blocks are just that, with the intention to stop the force of the attack first, then draw through the target. The following series of six blocks completes one drill. Economy of motion will dictate whether a hack or a slice can be used.

This drill is detailed from a right-handed grip. Work it with the left hand also. Just reverse the angles.

1) Blade edge crosses your body from the right to the left side, to hack/block an opponent's right attack. The blade tip is down. The blade could hit any part of the attacker. It could strike the weapon, or the limb. Your body zones to the right.

2) Blade edge turns out to your right side and the left side of the opponent, to hack/block an opponent's left attack. Remember to accentuate the turning out of the hand, accentuating the knuckles. Your body zones to the left.

3) Sweeping to block the opponent's lower right side attack. Your blade tip should be pointed downward. Your body zones to your right.

4) Sweeping hack/block vs. a lower left side attack. Your body zones to the left.

5) Blade edge high, in a upward hack/block vs. an overhead attack. The blade should intercept any downward attack and the backup hand pushes it off to the side.

6) Downward or horizontal block, covering the centerline of the body.

1

2

3

4

5

6

# Drill 3: Arm Stop/Block Drills

An arm or shoulder stop-block is used almost exclusively in close-quarter fighting, as an in-tight, reflexive reaction against:

a) a high hooking punch/attack or any high horizontal fist,

b) a high, hooking, stabbing knife attack that travels the same path as a wide-angle punch.

A big, wide, swinging, hooking punch attack, chambered from the back

**Basic breakdown of the shoulder stop**

In empty hand fighting, the shoulder stop is a straight line assault vs. a wide angle assault. The stop fires onto the lower deltoid area of the attacking arm, fired in the first 25 percent of the attack. Used any later during the arm attack and the opportunity, or opening, to the shoulder does not exist. The stop can be a palm strike, or a fist. The palm acts more as a stopper/catcher than the fist, the first being an impact assault.

Palm block to bend

The arm stop attacks the bend of the incoming arm. This short-circuits the energy of the opponent's hand, whether it is a fist or holds a knife. Catching too high on the arm, or too late in the swing, will probably mean the hooking attack will curl around your block and land! A early intercepted hooking punch is best stopped or blocked by a palm, not a fist, to the attacking shoulder.

Palm strike to shoulder

Vertical fist to bicep

Reverse grip hack block to arm

If you are holding a knife, and whether it is held in a saber or reverse grip, you execute the knife-hand block as you would execute a vertical fist punch. Either the knuckles of the fist or the edge of the blade will strike the target.

When executing the arm or shoulder stop-block, the practitioner should keep the free hand up in the window of combat, ready for action.

**Practice drill**

In this drill, the trainer holds two knives. The trainee holds one. Make sure the stop/block is executed at the proper time, early in the attack swing.

Saber grip hack block to arm

**Step 1:** the trainer throws a hooking style stab from the right and,

**Step 2:** the trainee blocks it with a blade to the bend of the attacking arm,

**Step 3:** the trainer throws a hooking style stab from the left side and,

**Step 4:** the trainee blocks it with a blade to the bend of the attacking arm,

**Step 5:** and so on . . . repeat the attacks and increase speed.

1

4

2

Execute this drill with these varables:

1) Right-handed saber grip
2) Left-handed saber grip
3) Right-handed reverse grip
4) Left-handed reverse grip

3

## Drill 4: Presas 12 Angle Blocking Combat Drills

This Presas 12 angle drill was detailed in a previous chapter. It is an excellent training skill-enhancing pattern. It must be memorized and can be fed to a training partner for a multitude of knife fighting responses. This one drill includes both slashing and stabbing, therefore giving a partner an opportunity to respond to both major styles of attacks. The Presas 12 angle drill will appear throughout this encyclopedia. Here is a review of those angles again.

**Angle 1:** Right-handed slash to the left side of the opponent's face;

**Angle 2:** Right-handed slash to the right side of the opponent's face;

**Angle 3:** Right-handed slash to the left side of the opponent's shoulder, bicep or rib area;

**Angle 4:** Right-handed slash to the right side of the opponent's shoulder, bicep or rib area;

**Angle 5:** Straight stab to the midsection;

**Angle 6:** Straight stab, knuckles inward, to the heart and chest;

**Angle 7:** Straight stab, knuckles outward, to the right side of the opponent's chest;

**Angle 8:** Low back slash to the right side of the opponent's thigh;

**Angle 9:** Low slash to the left side of the opponent's thigh;

**Angle 10:** Straight high stab, knuckles inward, to the opponent's left eye. You might grab the hair with your backup hand;

**Angle 11:** Straight high stab, knuckles outward, to the opponent's right eye. You might grab the hair with your backup hand;

**Angle 12:** A downward slash upon the side of the head or face, then a quick back stab under the chin.

**The blocking responses to the 12 angles**

The blocks will be studied through the three main possibilities:

Combat Response 1: Unarmed
Combat Response 2: Armed with a saber grip
Combat Response 3: Armed with a reverse grip

**Combat response 1: Unarmed slap block vs. the 12 angles**

a) Slap/block the hand/wrist through a series of 12

b) Slap/block the forearm through a series of 12

c) Slap block, grab and strike

Blocks are randonly sampled in the following photo series. Just remember to train by running each response through the 12 angles of attack.

Samples of blocking with empty hands

1

4

2

5

3

6

7

10

8

11

9

12

To block and strike vs. the 12 angles

1

3

2

4

5

6

7

## Combat response 2: Armed saber block the weapon limb

a) Hack/block the hand through a series.
b) Hack/block the forearm through a series.
c) Hack/block anywhere on the arm through a series.
d) Hack/block anywhere on the arm, and handstrike with the free hand through a series.

Blocks and responses are randomly sampled in this next photo series. Remember to run each response through the 12 angles.

1

2

3

4

5

6

7

8

## Combat response 3: Armed reverse grip block the weapon limb

a) Hack/block the hand through a series.

b) Hack/block the forearm through a series.

c) Hack/block anywhere on the arm through a series.

d) Hack/block anywhere on the arm and handstrike with the free hand through a series.

1

4

2

5

3

6

# Drill 5: Advanced Counter Attack Follow Ups

This series is perfect for solo practice. It develops coordination, speed, flexibility as well as aerobic conditioning.

## Saber grip series

Blocking through the 6 angle drill...

Series 1: Block and slash
Series 2: Block and stab
Series 3: Block and pommel strike
Series 4: Block and handstrike
Series 5: Block and kick
Series 6: Block and any of the above in combination

Right-handed and left-handed.

## Reverse grip series

Blocking through the 6 angle drill...

Series 1: Block and slash
Series 2: Block and stab
Series 3: Block and pommel strike
Series 4: Block and handstrike
Series 5: Block and kick
Series 6: Block and any of the above in combination

Right-handed and left-handed.

## Empty hand series

Using the empty hand blocking basics of...

a) Same-side block/grab
b) Cross the body and block/grab
c) Double-handed block/grab

Series 1: Block/grab and handstrike
Series 2: Block/grab and kick
Series 3: Block/grab and any combination

There is a Congress video "Knife Block and Counter Attack" that teaches many combat counter attack techniques off of empty hand, saber and reverse grip blocking.

## Chapter 12

# Knife Disarming

## The Basic Disarms

Knife disarms are both accidental and incidental in the encounter. You cannot affix a push/pull disarm in your mind as your specific goal while you stand before an armed opponent. If you are preoccupied with your push/pull disarm, you might miss a chance for a throat punch, or a different type of disarm. Keep an open mind to all opportunities. This chapter will detail each step in the following disarm strategies. Train your muscle memory in drills that relate to the following concepts.

Here are basic knife disarm categories.

### 1) Verbal disarms

If the circumstances dictate, one might be able to talk the opponent into dropping, re-sheathing or surrendering his weapon.

### 2) Impact disarms

a)  Long range weapons for impact: It is easier to blast or cut the weapon-bearing hand with any object you can find, the longer the tool, the safer and better.

b)  Short range weapons for impact: Blast with any tool or cut with any edged object, the weapon-bearing hand with any object you can find while in this range.

c) Impact the weapon-bearing hand, wrist, forearm, elbow, upper arm with your hand, knees, torso, etc. (I do not recommend trying, from opposing fighting stances, to kick a knife out of the hand of a sober and alert individual.)

### 3) Wristlock and X-pattern/wristlock disarms

This is when you rip, bend or twist the wrist severely enough to obtain a disarm. The X-pattern (not X-block) alone is not a disarm, but rather an intricate part of the wristlock that sets up the disarm.

### 4) Push/pull disarms

This is when you capture the weapon-bearing limb, pull while pushing on the blade, or pull on the blade and pushing on the limb.

Some experts would have you think that attempting to disarm someone with an edged weapon is suicide. Then they leave you with no option. I believe they take the position that anyone who might brandish a knife before you is Bruce Lee! Not so. I've done disarms, seen others do them, and read documented reports of many successful disarms! They can be done!

True, the knife, like the gun, is a great equalizer, however many people who brandish knives are drunk, or drugged, or uncoordinated and out of shape. Most have no idea how to fight.

Run, always run from the knife fight. But this chapter, like this whole encyclopedia, is based upon the premise that sometimes you can't! If the options are death to you and yours, or fighting for your life and having a chance, then this chapter will detail the skills needed to disarm the opponent.

All these disarm techniques and drills are demonstrated in Hock's knife fighting disarming concepts video.

## Verbal Disarms

The study of disarming techniques must begin with the art of verbal persuasion, or in some cases, pleading. Like a salesman cannot always use the same approach with each and every new customer, there is no one universal way to convince someone into surrendering their knife. The main strategy is to try and assess the attacker's motive. Sometimes the attacker verbalizes his intent immediately. From there you must snap-judge some responses.

Again, there are basic situations:

1) You are armed.
2) You are unarmed.

from which...

3) The attacker wishes to rob you.
4) The attacker wishes to rape you.
5) The attacker wishes to scare you off.

6) The attacker wishes to shock and/or intimidate you.
7) The attacker wishes to take revenge for something you've done.
8) The attacker wishes to kidnap you.
9) The attacker wishes to coerce you into admitting or revealing something.
10) The attacker is crazy and has no understandable motive.
11) The attacker wishes to kill you.

You must first determine what the motive of the attacker is. Sometimes you must figure this out. Once you do, then you can begin your attempts at verbal disarming.

**Verbal disarm approach 1: Air of surrender**
"Okay, Okay! You don't need to use that. Put away the knife, man. I am not going to fight you. I am leaving. I am no threat."

"Okay! Here is my wallet. Here is my jewelry. I am leaving it on the ground. Put away the knife. Here is what you want."

**Verbal approach 2: Air of hopelessness**
"You are not going to get away with this. The police are near. They will hunt you down, if you do this to me. For the rest of your life you will be running, a fugitive or you will be in jail!"

"Can't you see the witnesses around here. You won't get away with this."

**Verbal approach 3: Air of fright**
"Come on, I'll kill YOU! I'LL KILL YOU! COME ON!"

"I am armed, and you are armed. Most likely we will both die here today in this fight. Are you prepared to die today?"

"I am a trained (soldier, martial artist, police officer, boxer, knife fighter, whatever). You do not want to go up against me."

**Verbal approach 4: Air of self-doubt**
"Can you kill me? Can you really do it? Can you live with this? I don't think you can."

## "Defang the Snake" Impact Disarms

In many Filipino martial arts, there is a concept called "Defanging the Snake" in a fight. The venomous bite from the fang of the snake is the most deadly. Without the fangs, the bite is harmless. This translates to knife fighting.

The disarming impact can come from a tool such as a stick, or from another knife, or empty handed (the least effective but still sometimes the only option). You must impact the weapon-bearing hand, wrist, forearm or upper arm of the opponent, taking away his most deadly weapon, the "fang" or blade. This is a vital battle-plan.

This impact section in knife disarming will cover:

1) advantages to impacting the weapon-bearing limb,
2) long range impact disarms,
3) medium range impact disarms,
4) Presas 12 angles skill developing drills,
5) blade slap impact disarm,
6) "Don'ts," long and short range impact disarm mistakes.

There are many advantages to concentrating on the knife hand as a primary target.

**Advantage 1)** A hit, slash or hack on the knife hand can completely destroy the fingers and/or grip on the knife. A cut on the inside of the forearm can destroy the finger control, and thus, the grip on the knife.

**Advantage 2)** A hit, slash or hack can cause numbness in the grip hand.

**Advantage 3)** A bleeding wrist or forearm slice can saturate the knife hand with blood. If the knife hand is below the cut, gravity and/or momentum forces the blood onto the hand, making the opponent's grip slippery.

### The three ranges
### 1) Long range impact disarms
Defanging, impact disarms can be done from a long range with a long weapon that can be swung and controlled with quickness, such as a stick.

### 2) Medium range impact disarms
Defanging impact disarms can be done in the medium range with a shorter object such as with a short stick or a knife. In a knife vs. knife disarm scenario, the best disarm is executed with your blade, be it a slash or a severe hack.

Defanging impact disarms can also be done in medium range with a hand or forearm strike.

### 3) Short range impact disarms
Impact disarms are most effective in the long and medium range. In the shortest of ranges, belly-to-belly with the opponent, economy of combat motion may dictate

that you strike at the throat rather than twist your body around to cut the knife-hand first. This will be discussed later in this section.

**Presas skill developing drills**

The Presas 12 angles of attack drill has been detailed in several of the prior chapters, and is an excellent way to drill impact and slashing disarms, commonly called "destructions." In terms of knife vs. knife fighting, a knife destruction might be a slash or hack that lessons the power and movement of the weapon-bearing limb, yet does not always complete a disarm.

**Target training for the 12 angle drill**

1) the actual weapon
2) the hand
3) the wrist
4) the forearm
5) the upper arm

Impact on hand

Impact on wrist

Impact on forearm

Impact on weapon

Impact on bicep

## Drill series 1: Stick vs. knife

Versus the 12 angles of attack, hit the above listed targets of the knife-wielding trainer with the trainee's stick.

## Drill series 2: Knife vs. knife

Versus the 12 angles of attack, hit the listed targets.

Refer to Chapter 16's skill-developing Hubud drill for more study in defanging impact slashes.

## Drill series 3: Empty hand vs. knife

Versus the 12 angles of attack, strike with a hand or forearm, the above listed targets. You might exclude striking the blade as a target. This sounds like common sense, but I know of some martial artists who drill the split-second skill of hitting the side of the blade. Remember to train left arm impacts and right arm impacts.

## The blade slap impact disarm

A consummate knife fighter should be practiced and familiar with this disarming strategy. In that all knife disarms are dangerous, this disarm is particularly dangerous because one-half of the movement requires you to slap/impact the side of the knife blade. It should only be executed after you have analyzed several factors. The scenario it fits best in, is when the opponent displays a knife before you in an offending and threatening manner. It should come at a time when the opponent is more busy with his threatening words than concentrating on the knife he is brandishing.

If you can make this assessment of your opponent, and he puts a blade before your face in the appropriate range, this blade slap disarm may work. It is a "now he has it, now he doesn't" disarm that strikes like lightening.

There are three major considerations to this disarm, the grip, the angle the blade is held, and the height of the blade before you.

a) Look to see if the opponent has a "death grip" on the handle.

You can tell this by the tension in the forearm if it is exposed, or tension in the hand and fingers. Look to see if the thumb is wrapped tightly around the handle. Look to see if the blade is at a 90-degree angle from the wrist, the typical grip of a hammering or blocking strike. If the grip is tight, you might not be able to slap it free.

The disarm will be most effective if the opponent is holding the knife in a Filipino style grip, slightly canted forward in the hand.

b) Check out the angle that the opponent is holding the knife. Is the knife tip higher than the wrist? Can you sufficiently and significantly slap a flat side of the blade, while your other hand slaps the hand and wrist area in the opposite direction?

c) The knife should be high enough that you can execute this double slap safely, without cutting your hand.

d) The double slap must be lightening fast.

**Step 1:** The opponent stands before you, holding the knife still and in a threatening manner. The knife blade should be vertical, that is, the edges straight up and down. For the purposes of this explanation, the knife is in his right hand. The knife could be canted forward before you, in about a 45-degree angle.

**Step 2:** You slap the side of the blade with the palm of your left hand, as you slap the inside of the knife-bearing hand with your right hand. This is like a clapping motion, but your hands do not collide. This should send the knife flying.

Another option might be to strike the wrist area with a knuckle punch style of attack. This hard impact may produce a reflexive snapping action on the knife hand and further the cause of the disarm.

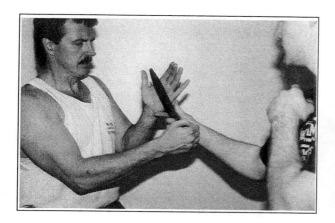

## The "don'ts": Long and short range impact disarm mistakes

A close range impact disarm may come after you have captured the weapon-bearing arm. You could fire a multiple knee strike to the limb.

We have discussed the "do's" of impact disarms. Now we must cover the "don'ts." Do always strike a smart and proper target. Do be in the proper range to complete a logical and successful destruction in a knife fight. Don't do the wrong thing in the wrong range.

If you pass a destruction opportunity to cut on the opponent's knife hand, and instead you jump in closer to cut his throat, you might be successful, but the opponent could still slash at you multiple times in the seconds before he becomes shocked or incapacitated from your attack as you lunge out of close range.

If you are extremely close to the opponent's torso, don't pass on a throat target to turn your torso and seek a defanging wrist slash. The opponent could get you in a choke, if you turn to defang.

When you are in close...

Don't turn to try an impact disarm...

It could get you into trouble.

Instead, trap and strike.

The opponent could also seize and control your weapon arm, if you turn to defang. Instead, maybe choose to wrap the weapon-bearing arm into a trap, and/or slashing the throat is a smarter option. This armbar wrap is very common in all types of realistic fighting.

Here, the weapon arm is wrapped and controlled long enough to attempt a deadly attack.

A survivor! The slap disarm demonstrated on page 166 worked! The opponent was disarmed and quickly knocked off his feet. The encounter over, our hero later received stitches in his hand.

His hand recovered completely. Your choice? Stitches or death? This disarm has worked against criminals and the defenders have been uncut!

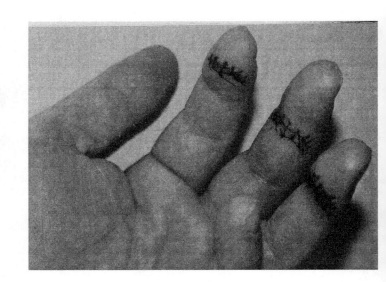

# Wristlock/X-Pattern Style Disarms

## The five basic wristlocks

The knife is held in the hand, and that hand is operated by the wrist. A fighter should learn that any tight, circular pressure forced and twisted upon the opponent's wrist in any direction, should cause pain. If this pain is sharp enough, the hand can loose control and drop the knife. This pressure can range from pain-compliance joint-locking, to bone, sinew and ligament damage, to sheer breaking. The joint damage or break can be caused by severely palm-striking or punching the back of the hand.

Many of these locks require the support of securing the next major joint, the elbow, either by cradling such as placing the elbow in the crook of the arm; or side support such as bracing the forearm beside your forearm, or by freezing the elbow against a wall or the ground.

Forearm brace

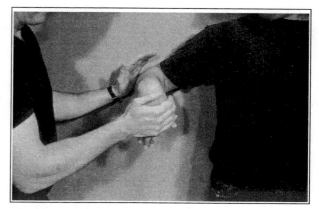
Wall brace

Floor brace

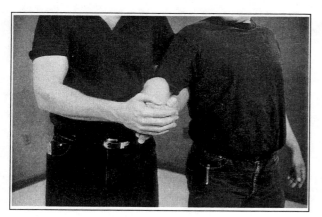
"Crook" of the arm brace

## 1) The palm in wristlock

This is when the palm of the hand is forced in the smallest circle to the forearm.

## 2) The "reverse" or "knuckle bender" wristlock

This is when the knuckles and the back of the hand are bent in the smallest circle possible, toward the outside of the forearm.

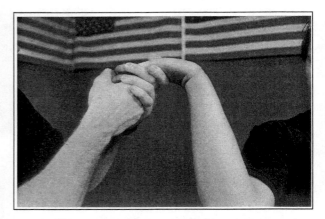

### 3) The "outer twist" wristlock

This is when the hand is twisted in the smallest circle possible to the outside of the opponent's body.

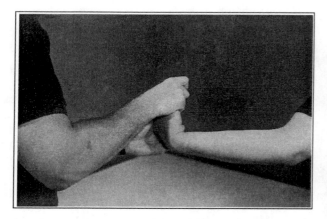

### 4) The "classical wristlock inner twist"

This is when the wrist is twisted in the smallest circle possible toward the front of the opponent's body. The opponent's elbow is twisted pointing upward.

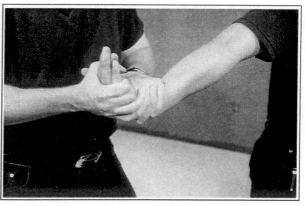

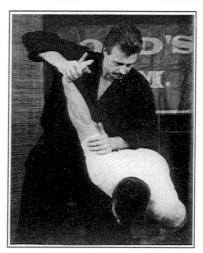

One follow-up response, the armbar wristlock takedown

## 5) The wrist pinch, the "V" lock or "S" lock

This is when the hand and wrist, and even the arm, is shaped into an "S," and severely pinched to the side. This can be bent against the joint horizontally or vertically.

Understand now that no matter what direction you might even thoughtlessly and violently twist an opponent's wrist, you will automatically engage in one of these wristlocks.

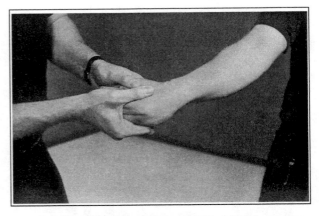

# The Chaos Wrist-Ripper Disarm Drill

Given the previous section's study in attacking the wrist, this drill puts it all in action.

The attacker feeds the 12 angles of attack, and you respond by seizing the hand and wrist in both hands. You will simulate snapping or ripping the knife hand in any direction that the attacking energy comes in. There should be no pre-planned steps to the response other than snatching and snapping the wrist, and that is where the term "Chaos" comes in. It also reaps chaos on the opponent's wrist.

This can be a dangerous drill to practice intensely. Before beginning, your partner might loosen up his wrist joint and remain relaxed throughout the drill, or wear a brace.

In reality, this is meant to severely damage the joint of the knife attacker.

If your opponent appears very muscular, with strong forearms and wrists, you might change strategies.

Catch...

Rip the joint

Catch...

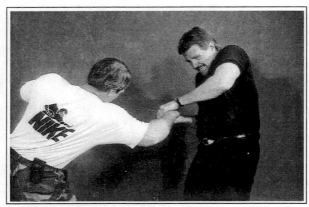

Rip the joint

## Advanced training drill

Acquire the hand and wrist catch, snap and/or rip, then kick and throw using the double handed grip.

## The elusive wristlock throat slash

Many martial artists like to demonstrate a throat slash after they acquire a basic outer wristlock. Usually before they execute the outer wristlock throw, they push the knife to the throat of the attacker, slash the far side of his throat, and then return the wristlock to a proper, safer height and turn the hand and wrist for the throw. This looks very flashy in demos and usually wows the audience, but the movement is dangerous without understanding the essentials involved.

Is the knife double-edged? If it is not double-edged, then you probably can't get the throat slash in. The dynamics of the hand twist etc. will probably turn the single-edged blade away from the throat when you try this trick.

As legend Walley Jay would say, "You must take out the play." When you are executing the basic wristlock and then the outer wristlock throw, you must lower the joint-lock to navel or hip level. This prevents the opponent from wriggling free of the joint-lock by maneuvering his elbow to either side. You take out the play in the elbow by dropping the wristlock low. If the joint-lock is high, then the opponent has much maneuver-ability in the elbow. A shoulder-high joint-lock offers your opponent many counters and escapes. Remember, your attempted throat slash is NECK HIGH! You might lay one of your forearms upon the closest forearm of the opponent while raising the lock to neck-height. This might take out some of the play.

If you think you might want to try this counter attack slash, you must use insert striking. Are you having trouble raising the joint-lock? Too much muscle resistance? Strike the bicep with the blade of your hand. A foot stomp on the instep usually shakes the opponent's concentration.

Inaccompanied Cello
Performed on Double

e, Domestic, Compact

Bach, Johann

ssical

Justin

JBF456@AOL.COM

## The Wristlock Disarm Progression Drill

These disarms involve wristlocks as the disarm, control and takedown responses to stabs. You must master the principles of wristlocks discussed in the previous strategy to make these work.

The X-patterns are used to "take out the play" after a block, setting up the snare of the weapon-bearing wrist.

The so-called "X-block" has become a controversial topic in knife defense, because a quick withdrawal of the opponent's knife during the traditional "X-block" could cut both your wrists. In these sets, the X-pattern responses are not classical X-blocks per say, that set up the wristlock disarms.

The quick retraction and cut

Please note that the way I acquire an X is not simultaneously. First, there is a single limb block, then a fast, snaring reach to the hand. Only a still photo might show a complete X, but the traditional "X" may never be in place.

Block...

The X-block

Then snare...

...and lock

The 6 angles of attack for this drill:
1) right-handed, torso stab
2) right-handed, torso stab
3) left-handed torso stab
4) left-handed torso stab
5) right-handed, knuckles inward high stab
6) left-handed, knuckles inward high stab

1

2

3

4

5

6

Blocks are most always facilitated with body evasion twisting or footwork. The actual contact blocks used in this drill are:

1) a low forearm block
2) a palm or slap block

Right! Your right leg must be safely out of the way of your low forearm block.

Wrong! You're knocking the blade right into your thigh.

The slap lock

There are three basic wristlocks executed in this drill:

1) Classical or basic wristlock
2) Outer wristlock throw
3) S-lock

Basic wristlock

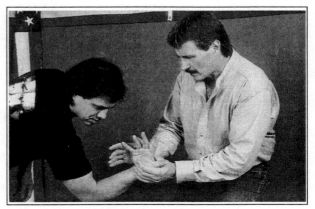

Outer wristlock throw

S-lock

These painful wristlocks greatly diminish the gripping power on the knife and allow for the follow-up disarm.

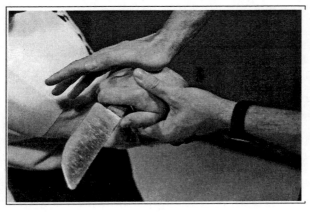

## X-pattern/wristlock disarms for numbers 1 and 4:

This set of two disarms works from a low inside to outside forearm block vs. a torso attack. The attacker can stab from his right or left to your mid-torso target in this set. You block with your forearm again and zone to the outside of the body. In this set of two techniques, you end up in an outer wristlock throw/disarm.

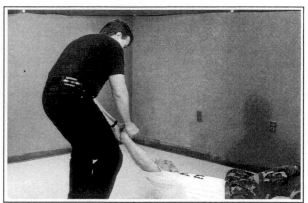

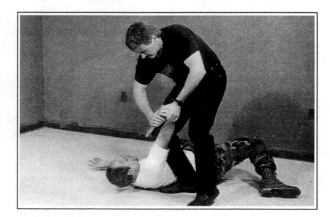

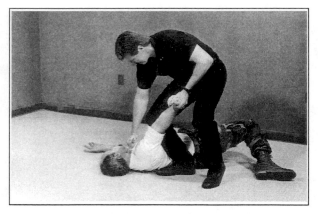

## X-pattern wristlock disarm responses numbers 2 and 3:

This set of two disarms concerns itself with a forearm, wrist or blade of the hand block from the inside to the outside, as you step to the inside of the encounter. In this set, the attacker can stab at your torso with his left or right hand.

Right stab:

a)  You block with the right forearm, or wrist, or blade of the hand. Economy dictates that you step to the center of the encounter.

b)  You reach with your left hand and snare the knife hand. Hook kick to the back of the opponent's right leg is optional, if needed.

c)  You twist the wrist into a basic or classical wristlock, causing his elbow to point upward.

d)  using the pressure on the wrist, rip the knife out of his hand with your "inside" hand and attack to the rear of the body.

If you attack to the front, the opponent might be able to use his free hand to block you.

Left stab:

Repeat the above steps from the opposite side.

4

1

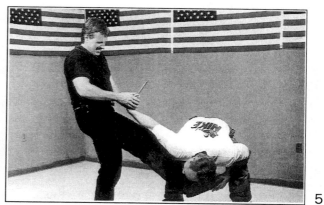

5

2

6

3

7

**X-pattern wristlock disarm responses numbers 5 and 6:**

This set of 2 disarms concerns itself with two higher line stabs, IF THE ATTACKER IS STABBING WITH HIS KNUCKLES INWARD, a commonly taught martial arts technique. If the knuckles are outward, you should not attempt this particular disarm.

High right stab:

a) Your right hand blocks.

b) Your left hand executes a clockwise attack upon the upper elbow, lower tricep part of the arm, making the X-pattern, and pushes the arm inward. Optional low-line kick.

c) Your right hand seizes the opponent's knife-bearing hand, its knuckles already inward.

   1) Your right hand is high on the weapon hand near the knuckles and fingers,

   2) Your left hand grips the upper forearm near the elbow and pulls it outward, creating a bend.

3) Keep the wrist higher than the elbow.

4) Turn the fingers of the hand back toward the opponent's face as if you are opening a jar to a spot beyond the opponent's nose. This causes a very painful pinch in the wrist.

5) Pull the overall arm downward.

6) Knee to the face.

d) You rip the knife from the weakened grip and counter-attack to the rear of the opponent.

High left stab:

   Repeat the above steps from the opposite side.

1

2

5

3

6

4

# The Push/Pull Disarm Progression

The purpose of this drill is to introduce to a student an overall disarming technique and its many variables. It is an exposure to possibilities. Master the drill and retain forever a versatile and valuable tool.

Never chase the push/pull disarm, or any disarm. It either will be there, or it won't be there. Your muscle memory must seize the moment during the chaos of a fight.

The following sequence of 12 push-pull disarms constitute one complete progression drill, and with the conceptual variations, explain the total opportunities for this disarm. Six of these disarms respond to a right-handed attack, six respond from a left-handed attack, totaling 12 disarms.

Many knife-fighting experts and martial artists teach this type of disarm, but they demonstrate them in disjointed ways. You might never grasp the overall fundamentals. I want you to learn the push/pull concept! Once you grasp the concept, and work through the drill, you will learn this progression and never forget the 12 disarms.

These disarms progress up the arm, are executed with your weapon, hand, forearm and tricep to the attacking blade. All are predicated upon grasping the opponent's knife-gripping thumb with your backup hand. All are executed by zoning "outside" of the opponent's attacking arm. The disarm is executed with a push upon the blade, and a pull upon the opponent's thumb and hand.

## The pulling force

Once you obtain the grip upon the thumb area of the opponent's hand, you pull in. This pull can be straight brute force, or it can be a nuisance that helps the upcoming push. When you pull in, try to pull in such a manner as to create a bend or pinch in the wrist. This bend usually helps to reduce finger-gripping strength.

## The pushing force

Pushing is a mild word in these circumstances. Blasting is a better term to describe the explosion needed to eject the knife from the hands of a fighter. In training you might push, but in a real fight, blast through the blade.

After zoning to the outside of the knife attack, and obtaining a thumb grip, you begin.

The pushes are:
1) your knife blade to the flat of the knife blade,
2) your palm, thumb down, and pushes, not necessarily grabs, the lower part of the knife,
3) your backhand to the flat of the knife blade,
4) your forearm to the flat of the knife blade,

5) your elbow to the flat of the knife blade,

6) your fist, then your forearm blasts through the side of the knife to land on the face. The opponent's knife-hand must be slightly bent inward at the wrist for this to be a smart tactic. This might be a response to a hooking style stab.

The naive might shriek at the thought of executing number 2. Pushing against the side of the blade is indeed dangerous, but remember the survival concept of minimizing the potential injury to yourself. Should the opportunity to execute this disarm occur, don't pass it up! A cut on the hand is better than a sliced and diced throat later, should the fight continue.

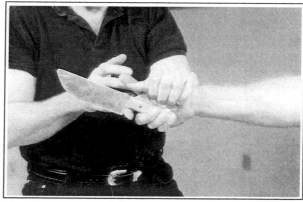

The thumb acquisition

**Push/pull disarm 1: Knife push vs. knife**

You are armed. You catch and grip the opponent's knife hand with your free hand, grabbing the thumb of that hand. This alone reduces the opponent's knife grip. Then put the flat of your knife blade against the flat of your opponent's knife blade. Pull in the free hand, force out the knife from the opponent's hand, simultaneously.

Zone away from the attack

### Push/pull disarm 2: Palm push vs. the knife

You are unarmed. You catch and grip the opponent's knife hand with your left hand, and with your thumb down, your right hand palms the blade and pushes. After the opponent's control is lost, you can grab the blade, or you can let it eject.

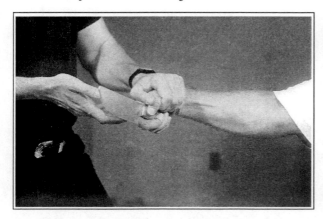

### Push/pull disarm 3: Back of the hand push vs. the knife

You catch and grip the opponent's knife hand with your free hand, grabbing the thumb of that hand. This reduces the opponent's knife grip. Then you put the back of your hand against the flat of the blade, pull in with your gripping hand and force your backhand out simultaneously. (This can be executed while you hold your own knife, or a gun, or anything.)

Wrong! Blade cuts the hand.

Right! Blade is sideways and flat against the hand.

### Push/pull disarm 4: Forearm push vs. the knife

You are armed or unarmed. You catch and grip the opponent's knife hand with your free hand, grabbing the thumb of that hand. This reduces the opponent's knife grip. Then you put your forearm against the flat of the blade, pull in with your gripping hand and force your forearm out, simultaneously. This can be executed while you hold your own knife, or a gun, or anything. Should you hold a knife, you can slash the opponent as you force your forearm outward for the disarm.

### Push/pull disarm 5: Elbow or upper arm push vs. the knife

You are armed or unarmed. You catch and grip the opponent's knife with your free hand, grabbing the thumb of that hand. This reduces the opponent's knife grip. Then you put the back of your elbow or upper arm against the flat of the blade, pull in with your gripping hand and force your elbow or arm out, simultaneously. Again, this can be executed while you hold your

knife, or a gun, or anything. Should you be armed with a knife, you can sometimes be in range to slash the opponent as you force your forearm outward for the disarm.

### Push/pull disarm 6: Punch vs. the knife

You are armed or unarmed. If you can get the gripped wrist to bend in, all the better for the above disarms. But this bent-wrist position coupled with a wide opponent's blade, allows for a unique disarm opportunity. Turn the blade sideways, and punch through the blade into the face.

the opponent's thumb and knife-hand, with the push/pull technique, could produce a disarm.

## Push/pull disarm conceptual variations:

a) Other body parts: It would stand to reason that other body parts, for example—knees or thighs, lats, hips, etc.—forced against the flat blade of the knife, aided by a solid hand hold on

## Counters:

There is one major counter to these dis-arms:

a)  Switch hands counter: Switching hand strategies were detailed earlier in this encyclopedia. Here is a classic example where they work. When you feel the blade coming out of your hand, grab it with your other hand and counter attack.

## Advanced training drill

Where possible, after pushing the blade free of the opponent's grip, take your pushing hand and follow-up with a slapping strike, usually to the face.

...And so on through the 12 progressions

# The Reverse Grip Push/Pull Series

This push/pull disarm is effective when the attacker is holding the knife in a reverse grip and is stabbing inward or backhanded and downward at you from overhead, or at least bicep height attack.

The four angles of attack in this drill are:

1) right-handed side angle
2) right-handed high back hand
3) left-handed side angle
4) left-handed high backhand

## The basic block is:

A Kempo, karate, or Tae Kwon Do style block. You block from the same side as the attack. Right-handed attack is stopped with a left forearm. Left-handed attack is stopped with a right forearm. This block might be called a traditional "Judan Uke" or "Age Uke." It fires up in a straight line or an arcing half-circle to stop the attack, but ends in an angle. In this progression, the forearm block lodges between the blade and the opponent's forearm.

## Angles 1 and 3 responses:

The forearm stops or deflects the attack. You "palm" the bend of the arm, then slide your palm around the upper arm until your palm reaches the lower tricep. This snaking action is coupled with maneuvering the captured arm counterclockwise while you raise your elbow. The flat side of the blade should be upon your forearm. Continue the circular pattern until the blade is dislodged from the grip. Pull up on the upturning elbow with your free hand if you need assistance. Kicks and eye-jabs are, of course, optional, to distract and assist the movement.

2

**Angles 2 and 4 responses:**

These are responses to the high line back-hand attacks. If the attack comes in from a right high backhand, your right forearm blocks. You snake your right hand over the top of the bend of the opponent's arm, and keep snaking until the blade grip is lost. Reverse the process from the high left attack.

3

1

4

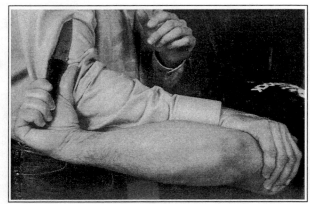

Close-up of disarm

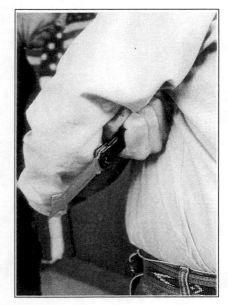

Close-up of disarm

Practice these exactly as I have described them. Your reflexive block against a high attack can turn into this effective counter. At worst, you may take a slice on the forearm. But you are still alive. I have executed these strip disarms against live blades in classes, seminars and on live television and have come to place great trust these motions. The have only been injured when a new training partner was fearful of attacking me with a real knife and delivered the knife in an unrealistic position. Watch out for that as you practice.

## Summary

It might be hard to estimate at the beginning of the chapter, but we have covered over 150 knife disarm techniques. It doesn't seem like that because I have organized them into categories and concepts/strategies. If you can grasp one basic concept/strategy, a multitude of disarms fall into place. Understanding and training turns to reflex. And that is why I must tell you this disarm story.

In 1973, I attended the Military Police Academy in Fort Gorden, Georgia. It was "old-school" Vietnam era training and the best police school I have ever attended. The last week of the Academy, we underwent "MP City." This is the final testing grounds. For five days, we attended a daily briefing, then with a partner, and a scorer/instructor, got in a jeep, and patrolled a part of Fort Gorden that was designated the training area. We answered realistic calls for service of all types. The victims, witnesses, and bad guys were volunteers from other Army units and they took their acting performances very seriously. Making the rookies look bad was their sport. Each scenario was a mandatory part of training. Each team/unit, for example, went to a full-blown bar fight at the "Bravo Club," a theft investigation, a violent domestic, etc.

One of the dispatched calls was to contact a crazy soldier wandering the streets. We stopped and approached the rather stout soldier. As I got close, he yanked out a knife (dull metal) and attacked me with a stab to the chest. Thanks to my Kenpo background, I took him down in a flurry of which, I still cannot recall exactly what I did, other than it involved catching the arm, a throw and disarm. My untrained-in-the-martial-arts partner hadn't yet as much as moved, until after I floored the bad guy.

I heard stories at the end of the week from the other rookies about what a rough encounter they had with that soldier. He "killed," "cut" and/or escaped from several of them.

Years later, I took knives and other weapons like hammers or bats from suspects. I even wrestled a loaded shotgun from an angry husband in one domestic.

Some of those times, I cannot recall exactly what techniques I used. That is reflex.

Still, somehow that soldier with the training knife rattled me more than any of these other real encounters. Maybe because it seemed like my first police fight. At that moment, the reality of the training, the resistance given by the soldier, and the flash of the knife was as real to me as if my life were truly at risk. The adrenaline rush left me shaking. My subsequent report was scribble.

In all my encounters since, winning some and then losing some too, for some reason, I have not been as shaken as that training day at the MP Academy over 20 years ago! I guess that old adage rings true, "The more you sweat in here, the less you bleed out there!"

Realistic training can prepare you for the real thing. It can give you muscle memory, reflex, and confidence. Practice these disarms. Disarms can work!

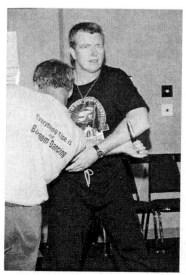

You must use whatever is in your environment to win a knife fight, or any fight for that matter. Often instructors will declare, "You can't disarm me! It is impossible!" But what if I bounced a lamp or a chair off their head? Suddenly, against a stunned opponent, knowledge of disarms can be very effective. Remember in the 1999 London, England knife attack on Beatle George Harrison, George took a shallow stab, but fought his stalker off. His wife smashed a lamp over the criminal's head! He was knocked senseless and they took the knife. Now that is an impact disarm! All across the world, every week, untrained people are disarming knives from bad guys with various degrees of success. If you can't run and you have to fight...go down fighting! You may never have to go!

# Chapter 13

# Support Handstriking and Kicking

### Skill and Knowledge 1: Empty Hand and Kicking Support

Handstriking and kicking play a crucial part in a knife fight. A novice may pick up a knife and be fixated upon its sole use, forgetting that his or her free hand and two legs are also potential weapons. A consummate knife fighter is also a skilled hand-to-hand fighter. A skilled knife fighter will pick up the knife and maximize its use with an arsenal of support hand, elbow, footwork and leg attacks to fake, feint, disrupt and devastate.

Since the days of the warring Samurai, weaponry was formally taught first, and empty hand fighting was considered the last resort confrontation on the battlefield, after all other weapons, the bow, the spear, the sword, the knife, were all broken or lost. Most Filipino martial art systems teach weaponry first, using the stick and the knife as tools to improve speed, timing, strength and coordination. These skills are then transferred over to the empty hand. This is usually the opposite of many current Asian and American fighting systems, who save the weapons for advanced levels.

Volumes of books and centuries of research have been discoursed about unarmed fighting. People have devoted their lives to these pursuits. I obviously cannot cover every aspect in this, a knife fighting encyclopedia. But the basic concepts of motion, energy, and physics, the elements that create the dynamics of hand-to-hand fighting as they relate to knife fighting, can be examined and drilled.

Survival fighting does not advocate the submission holds of grappling, nor does it promote point-tournament contests. Submission and point fighting were created to augment these skills, but often these rules of play interfere with the muscle memory of survival. Fundamentally, true survival, hand-to-hand fighting consists of:

1) striking as in handstrikes and kicks;
2) jointlock attacks;
3) throws and takedowns;
4) chokes;
5) groundfighting that emphasizes striking, breaking and choking.

This chapter deals with the "backup hand" techniques and empty hand techniques vs. the knife. Only the complete study of a common sense, reality-based martial art can put you on this total path that I hope to guide you along. The next section will help guide you to such a system. The following chapters define handstriking and kicking, related drills, and the best knife and backup hand exercise workout you will find anywhere!

These exercises, techniques, and drills are demonstrated in Hock's knife fighting video series.

## Skill and Knowledge 2: Hand-to-Hand Fighting School

To become a consummate knife fighter, you must understand and study the dynamics of hand-to-hand fighting. Where do you go to learn?

As a martial arts instructor, I've heard this scenario hundreds of times from walk-in-wannabes. It goes like this: man or woman sees Steven Segal, Cynthia Rothrock, Jackie Chan, or any martial arts movie. They want to learn how to fight like stars. They want to beat up the bad guys, save lives and rescue the politically-correct world? Where do they go to learn? One day this person drives down the street and spots a neighborhood karate or Tae Kwon Do school (as prolific as Seven-11s). Oh, he or she has cruised past the place a million times, but this time, the sign emits a mystic "Segalistic" message after seeing the latest movie. It's all karate, right Steven?

Three months later (if the student lasts that long), barefoot and in "white pajamas," they are screaming to match staccato motions. Fists poised on their hips, they ask, "How come Mike Tyson never pulled his fist way back on his hip between punches when he won all those championships?" and, "Tyson doesn't practice this way." With legs cranked far enough apart to titillate a Spanish inquisitor, they realize, "Segal doesn't stand like this!" And they wonder about all these katas, these dance things? "Did Iron Mike do all this fu-fuing around like a ballerina?"

When will they learn to street fight like Steve baby, or like the cops in *Lethal Weapon 3*? So our hero becomes disgruntled. Frustrated. Is all karate like this? They weren't interested in the "artsy," ancient stuff. They quit, and they don't really know why. Now you will learn how not to make the same mistakes!

## Be Consumer Aware

Basically, our friends are not consumer aware. They did not know that karate is to the martial arts as baseball is to athletics. Karate is just one element. "Martial arts" is a generic, international term representing armed and unarmed fighting systems and styles. They did not know that there are over 400 different kinds of Kung Fu! That countries like Africa, Russia, Greece, the Philippines and France, to name a few, have their own martial arts? While Korea, China and Japan might have a marketing monopoly, here in the U.S., they are far from the only Meccas of the fighting world! Our hero didn't shop for a martial arts school like they would have for a car part, a pizza or a even a haircut. Some homework would have disclosed the following, key decision-making facts.

First, decide what you want to learn. You don't learn how to play baseball by studying football. Figure out why you want to learn the martial arts. Is it for the art? Tournament competition? Street fighting self-defense? There are distinct differences.

What are the differences? Training to be a tournament "point" fighter will produce trophies, but not maximize muscle memory into that of a savvy, biting, scratching, eye-jabbing street survivor. I can recall a long-term karate student who reflexively bowed before a street fight and took a punch to the head from some untrained bully. True story! Muscle memory! For years he had bowed before each and every encounter and point match.

Studying the beautiful, graceful and aesthetic martial arts can push your own personal physical envelope, but won't win in the tougher point-fighting arena. In tournaments, I have seen kickboxers routinely decimate esoteric practitioners.

Take care to note that in America, to the ignorant, its all "karate," but karate is as different from Jujitsu as baseball is to football. Though baseball and football athletes possess common dominator motor skills, so too will martial artists. But their tasks, and skills are goal-specific. Learn the differences and be goal-specific in your selection.

# How to Select a School

## The traditional model

A good traditional school concerns itself with the perpetualization of history, of ancient respect, regimentation, the passing on of katas, and the handling of ancient weapons. Uniforms, called gis (pronounced like gees) are a must. Belts or sashes are achieved. Students are usually barefoot. There is bowing; foreign flags are displayed and foreign languages referenced. Usually, it's the teacher's main goal to produce a replica of himself and his instructors before him. Whatever fighting creativity there is, is usually found in non-curriculum training. Typically, a Japanese school is called a dojo (dough-joe), a Chinese school a Kwoon, and a Korean school a dojang (dough-john). Some such systems are Tae Kwon Do, most karate, Gung Fu or Kung Fu, and most styles of Aikido, Jujitsu and Judo—that is to say, Asian arts.

## The competition model

These are often not too different in look from most traditional schools, unless it is a western boxing or generic kickboxing class. Many schools believe that the ultimate fighter is really a trophy-winning competition kickboxer, and their training and sparring centers around ring fighting with referee rules. Uniforms are usually required, with a heavy dependence on gloves, foot pads, etc. Students bow, and there are usually foreign flags and foreign lingo.

Tae Kwon Do, karate, then Thai boxing or regular boxing, some Kung Fu, are just some of the systems that train primarily for competition. Of course, these skills do relate to street fighting, but often in an abstract way, and can actually create very bad street fighting habits.

There are some schools promoting grappling competition, that will have students performing a type of "college wrestling" where the superior goal and technique is a match-winning submission hold. There are people who love to do only this, and that is fine, providing you, as a consumer, know what you are getting into. Many of these people can tie you into a pretzel, but can't punch there way out of a paper bag.

Warning! Don't be fooled for a moment into thinking that these aerobic kickboxing workouts, so popular now, can in any way substitute for street fighting or competition training.

## The self-defense model

A good self-defense school concerns itself with EQUAL training time in the four combat ranges of a real street fight. Un-armed, the first range is the kicking range. Closing in, the next is the hand-striking range. Then, even closer to the trapping or immobilization of the opponent's limbs, to finally the grappling/groundfighting range. While any one of these ranges can be a means to an end, these four capsulize a real fight from start to takedown finish, all with no holds-barred, dirty, gutter techniques, and a good self-defense school emphasizes this.

There are no uniform requirements. Usually t-shirts, shorts or sweatpants and athletic shoes are recognizable hallmarks of such non-traditional groups. No flags. These schools could be called anything, usually, "Progressive Fighting...," "Modern ...this or that," or "Joe Blow Martial Arts." They are found in community centers, halls, gyms, etc. These institutes are geared to produce a '90s real-world warrior. Some such systems are Jeet Kune Do, Modern Filipino Arnis/Kali, Modern Pentjak Silat, or hybrid styles created by instructors toward this goal.

## A Few "Buyer Bewares"

1) Fundamental Tae Kwon Do is primarily a kicking art. Feet! Feet! Feet! (You could find yourself picking your nose with your toes when your fingers would work just fine or better, thank you very much!) Many TKD schools are overly concerned with instructing kids—teaching forms, katas, and hosting tournaments—so they can pay their bills.

2) Fundamental karate has now become primarily kicking and punching. Most karate is not known for fluid motion or for excellence in grappling and groundfighting.

3) Fundamental Jujitsu is a grappling art, and it can get "over-sporty" in certain schools. I am aware of some Jujitsu schools that will do only token punching and kicking to appear as a "complete" fighting system, but spend most of their training time on the mats acting like collegiate wrestlers.

4) Judo is a mat, hands-on, grappling SPORT. No dirty fighting allowed. Like a soccer player who forgets he has hands, a judo player can forget to kick, bite, strike and rip. Judo is dependant upon extra re-enforced uniforms for throwing and choking, therefore many of its techniques won't work well with tank tops or street shirts).

5) O Sensei Oeshiba Aikido schools and their splinter downline operations are designed to be spiritual journeys, with only abstract self-defense techniques. (It is commonly thought that what Segal does in the movies is Aikido, but Segal has black belts in different systems, and his cinema fighting is more of an aggressive combination of street fighting, Aiki-Jutsu, karate, a combat free-for-all.)

6) A good athlete can make a bad system look good. Look to the philosophies and fundamentals of the system, not to its premier athlete or instructor, to see its truths.

## Instructors

And speaking of individual athletes, let's talk instructors. Interview one as you would select an athletic coach. Braggarts, dummies, hot shots and shallows are out! Maturity and focus is in. And trophies do not the teacher make. The greatest self-defense instructor may not have trophy one! But a casual enquiry into his life experiences may reveal a lot. He might be a combat veteran, or a decorated cop with road-tested techniques.

Also, make sure the instructor is at least aware of modern sports and athletic training and development theories. For example, in some traditional Gung Fu, practitioners stand like a statue for 30 or more minutes in a painful, super-wide legged pose. This is supposed to create "stance power." A modern trainer would simply prescribe three sets of weight-lifting squats to get even better results. Now, if you are the eternal "artist," you might prefer the old way. And then again, you might find it a waste of time and head straight for the weight rack. The leg strength ends up the same!

Of course there are exceptions to the schools and instructors. Don't just discount a traditional school! The kicking instructor might have added the four-combat range program to satisfy the street fighters. That modern-looking karate dojo around the corner might cherish some of the traditions that would make you comfortable and happy. That traditional Jujitsu school may be introducing Wing Chun trapping hands to compensate for that system's lack of fighting skills in that range, to improve their entry techniques. And that iconoclastic, radical self-defense instructor in sweat pants probably has a black belt or two in his closet, and I'll bet you'll even find a gi in there somewhere!

Investigate the school! Investigate the instructor! Our frustrated heroes we examined in the first paragraphs simply signed up at the wrong school. They wanted to be a street fighter and instead wound up in a very classical, artsy class. It should be plain to you by now that systems can be as different as baseball is to football. Enquire about these issues before signing on the dotted line. You CAN achieve that black belt, or trophy, that certification, or that self-confidence you desire, with the right instructor and a suitable school. Be consumer aware! You might even save the politically-correct world someday! Steven would be proud.

# Skill and Knowledge 3: The Backup Hand

One of the main things that separates a veteran knife fighter from a novice knife fighter is the vet's experience in properly utilizing the rest of his body as a weapon to assist the blade attack. The most important knife-support, body weapon is the "backup" hand, or the unarmed hand. The backup hand can be used in many ways:

a)  To punch and handstrike,
b)  Fake a motion to set up an attack,
c)  Guard or block incoming attacks,
d)  Grab or trap the opponent,
e)  Switching knife hands,
f)  Pushing or body manipulation,
g)  Can actually slap the opponent's knife out of his hand.

There is minimum safety concern about positioning a secondary hand, or so-called "weak-side," in an empty hand fight. But in a knife fight, one should be concerned with the secondary limb taking a cut or stab. The backup hand could be turned palm-inward through much of the encounter, which will automatically turn the fleshy part of your forearm and the bloody inside of your wrist away from an immediate strike.

**a) To handstrike**
The backup hand can assist the knife attack by punching, eye-jabbing or chopping at the opponent. Drills practicing this will follow later in this chapter.

**b) To fake a motion to set up an attack**
To get the opponent to flinch, one could fake an eye-jab. The opponent's arms may raise in response to the fake, opening up a low line attack. Remember to assess the speed of your opponent. If an opponent is naturally slow to respond to a fake or even a real attack, a fast-action fake may be wasted upon him. Give him time to react to the fake, then attack.

1

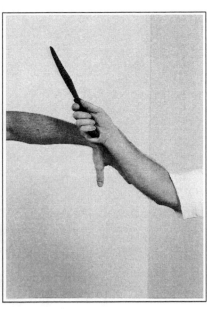

2

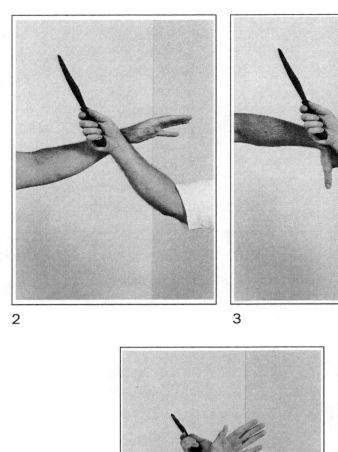

3

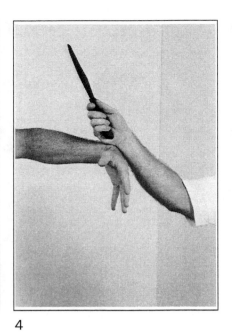

4

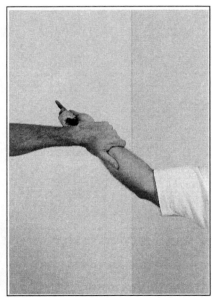

5

6

Meanwhile, between steps 5 and 6, you are already in the process of stabbing

## c) Guard or block incoming attacks

The backup hand can be used to block the opponent's backup hand or incoming knife hand.

## d) Grab or trap

The backup hand can grab the knife-holding arm or other arm, or as in disarms, grab the knife hand and fingers. The hair can be grabbed, the face, the clothing. A shirt or jacket lapel, the belt or beltline/pantline are good handles. A good fighter analyzes the clothing of his or her opponent. One cannot perform many Judo throws when the opponent is wearing a tank top. The grabbing hand can maneuver the opponent into your technique.

The backup hand can "trap" or immobilize the opponent. One example is an open palm upon the opponent's elbow to hold, just for a split-second, that arm into a position where a safer entry can be made.

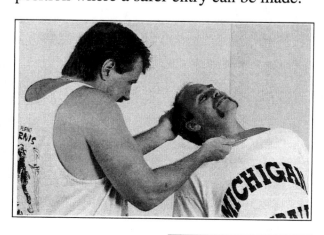

### e) Switch knife-hands

In the process of being disarmed, or when the knife-bearing hand is incapacitated, the fighter should switch hands and continue the fight. Some people like to switch knife hands for no other reason than to confuse the opponent. To each his own.

### f) Pushing and manipulations

The backup hand can push the opponent away. The hand can manipulate someone into position for attack.

It can push the opponent's body away, or—upon a stab—help pull a blade from a body. There are some traveling knife experts who strongly advocate this pushing of the body to pull out the knife after a stab. Obsessed with this, they more often neglect to cover the knife hand of the opponent, taking their backup and cover hand away from the opponent's weapon hand to do the pushing. Take care not to mimic this move. Utilize the blade-clearing body push only when the opponent is not armed or when it is safe.

## Skill and Knowledge 4: Hand Striking Techniques

Whether you have a knife in one hand, or you are fighting empty handed, a consummate warrior knows when to hit and how to hit hard and fast.

Punch too slow and have your punching arm struck—you have a bruise. Punch too slow and have your punching hand cut, and you may die from blood loss! Fighting with or against the knife offers a higher challenge to the fighter. Knife fighting handstrikes must land and rapidly retract to escape counter attack from the blade.

These handstrikes must be practiced and performed from a comfortable, modern, fighting stance, not a traditional, wide-legged horse stance. You do not have to memorize these handstrikes in this order, just familiarize yourself with them enough to:

a) shadow box for flow with authority and variety,

b) work a heavy bag for power with authority and variety,

c) spar for timing and target acquisition, with authority and variety,

d) finally, perform them all with your backup hand while you hold a knife in your other hand. Then switch hands.

1) Horizontal or boxer's punch

2) Vertical or karate punch

3) Back-fist

### 3) Back-fist, continued

### 4) Hooking punch

### 5) Hammer strike—the edge of the fisted hand

### 6) Palm strike

### 7) Eye jabs

8) Uppercut

9) Elbow strikes

## Skill and Knowledge 5: Kicking Techniques

The following section in our study will concern itself with a review of kicking. No study would be complete without an examination into the kicks of the martial arts systems. And the subject of kicking and instructional photographs could fill a whole, other, entire encyclopedia. Therefore we will only briefly review the subject.

### Kicking 1: Basic concepts in kicking

a) The power of kicks:

There are many advantages to kicking. Certainly, in the kicking range of combat, kicks are the primary weapons. First, your legs are more powerful than your arms. You use them in a variety of tasks daily, if even just walking around. Kicks often utilize the entire strength of the torso.

b) The length of kicks:

Your legs are longer than your arms, and therefore can strike while keeping vital body parts like your head at a safer distance from the opponent's weapons.

c) High kicks:

Landing a technical knock-out kick to the head is extremely difficult and unlikely in the real world of pants, shoes and unsteady ground and floor surfaces. It is even more dangerous when confronting a knife fighter, who will most likely slash open your leg with a reflexive block. Better to disable and distract the opponent from the waist down, for even the most uncoordinated novice has the reflexes to protect himself against objects flying in on the high line.

Bruce Lee once said, "I would no sooner kick a man in the head in a real fight, than bend over and punch him in the toe. It is not necessary." Once a practitioner moves into closer range, kicks share the responsibility of attack and defense, due to spacial limitations. Move too close, and they can turn into knee strikes.

d) The foot:

When using the foot as a weapon, one should strike an opponent with:

1) the top of the foot, or,

2) the bottom of the foot. The preference here is to kick with the flat of the foot striking the target in a horizontal impact. You can emphasize the heel as a weapon. This sets up good body positioning and gives the kicker more of a chance to make contact.

3) not with the side or blade of the foot! Striking with significant force with the blade of the foot could easily cause ankle damage. This approach is common in the martial

arts, but makes little to no sense. Can you walk down a flight of stairs with your feet twisted in, on the outside blades of your feet? Can you jump and land on the blades of your feet? Of course not. You will sprain or break your ankle. Why then kick with impact using the blade of your foot? I believe this foot edge can be safely and successfully used in low-power, flicking shin kicks, or low-line blocks or stop hits, where little power is used, but not with full power kicks.

e) No chambered kicks:

There should be as little "chambering," or to borrow from karate terminology—folding—as possible. For example, the classical, traditional front snap kick is a four beat exercise:

**Beat 1:** raise knee (the chambering or fold)

**Beat 2:** snap lower leg outward to kick

**Beat 3:** retract lower leg to folded knee position

**Beat 4:** lower knee and leg

While the street survival version is one beat:

**Beat 1/2:** The kick snaps up in a one beat. The knee and foot snaps up simultaneously.

**Beat 1:** The foot and knee returns simultaneously.

Even the classical people speed up their kicks in a fight with this split-second delivery.

f) Basic footwork that directly supports kicking:

There are specific kinds of footwork that support kicking.

1) Shuffle foot: This is usually when the rear foot pendulums up near the front foot, and the front foot executes a kick, often called a "displacement" of one foot by the other. The shuffle is like a skip. Then, depending upon the specific kick, the hips may be "squared off" such as in front kicks, or turned completely, such as in hook kicks.

2) Lunging footwork kicks: Lunge kicks close the distance to the enemy. The kicker's lunging foot "ricochets" off the floor, so as not to increase the speed involved in the kick. There are three reasons for executing a burning foot sidekick;

3) Hooking/pivoting footwork kicks: In many of the hooking style kicks, it is important to completely pivot the hips, so much so that the torso faces sideways from the opponent.

g) Faking:

1) You can sometimes set up a kick by either faking or actually striking out with your hands on the "high line." This draws the opponent's attention high, then strike on the "low line" by kicking.

2) You can fake with one kick and strike with another, usually from a different angle.

**Kicking 2: Basic kicks**
1) Front snap kick
2) "Combat" front snap kick (this curves in to the opponent's groin)
3) Back kicks
4) Side kicks
5) Hooking kicks
6) Stomp kicks
7) Oblique kicks
8) Spinning or turn kicks
9) Front thrust kicks

Practice kicking from a comfortable, modern, fighting stance, not a traditional, wide-legged horse stance. You do not have to memorize them in any order. You should be able to:

a) work the kicks out of right and left leads,

b) work the kicks off of the front and rear legs,

c) shadow box with authority and variety,

d) work them on a heavy bag for power and variety,

e) spar for timing and target acquisition with authority and variety,

f) finally, perform them all holding and interjecting a knife.

## Kicking 3: Kicking in a knife fight

I would like to report two important rules that should be followed as much as possible:

a) it is a sound idea to utilize low-line kicks in a knife fight. This keeps your legs away from the opponent's blade, and keeps you more mobile to escape his deadly attack.

b) never try to kick a knife out of a sober, alert opponent's hand, unless you are Superman.

Specific strategies using kicks in a sparring scenario can be found in Chapter 18.

## Skill and Knowledge 6: Basic Knife Support Exercises

This is where it all comes together, the kicking and the striking of the backup hand, working in conjunction with the knife hand.

To perform these exercises, stand in your selected fighting stance. Hold a knife in your selected hand. There are four steps in each set. Three of the steps in each set are from a saber grip. One step is a stab from the reverse grip. The slashes and hacks can come from any angle. These exercises should be worked in the four following ways:

a) in the air, like shadow-boxing;

b) hit a focus mitt or Thai pad held by a training partner;

c) hit a heavy bag;

d) actual knife sparring with an armed partner.

### Basic exercise series 1: Punching and knife work

Use vertical fist and/or horizontal fist or back-fist punches.

Punch with knife set 1: Slash and punch reps

Punch with knife set 2: Punch and slash reps

Punch with knife set 3: Hack and punch reps

Punch with knife set 4: Punch and hack reps

Punch with knife set 5: Stab and punch reps

Punch with knife set 6: Punch and stab reps

Punch with knife set 7: Reverse grip stab and punch reps

Punch with knife set 8: Punch and reverse grip stab reps

## Basic exercise series 2: The eye jab and knife work

Selected because of the eyejabs swiftness to enter and retract vs. the opponent's knife.

Eye jab and knife set 1: Slash and eye jab reps

Eye jab and knife set 2: Eye jab and slash reps

Eye jab and knife set 3: Hack and eye jab reps

Eye jab and knife set 4: Eye jab and hack reps

Eye jab and knife set 5: Stab and eye jab reps

Eye jab and knife set 6: Eye jab and stab reps

Eye jab and knife set 7: Reverse grip stab and eye jab reps

Eye jab and knife set 8: Eye jab and reverse grip stab reps

## Basic exercise series 3: Grabbing and knife work

Practice by lunging out to grab the top of a focus mitt, Thai pad or the arm of the trainer.

Grab and knife set 1: Slash and grab reps

Grab and knife set 2: Grab and slash reps

Grab and knife set 3: Hack and grab reps

Grab and knife set 4: Grab and hack reps

Grab and knife set 5: Stab and grab reps

Grab and knife set 6: Grab and stab reps

Grab and knife set 7: Reverse grip slash and grab reps

Grab and knife set 8: Grab and reverse grip stab reps

### Basic exercise series 4: Hooking kicks and knife work

Any hook kick, from the front leg or rear leg. Lower-line kicks are safer.

Hook kick and knife set 1: Slash and hook kick reps

Hook kick and knife set 2: Hook kick and slash reps

Hook kick and knife set 3: Hack and hook kick reps

Hook kick and knife set 4: Hook kick and hack reps

Hook kick and knife set 5: Stab and hook kick reps

Hook kick and knife set 6: Hook kick and stab reps

Hook kick and knife set 7: Reverse grip stab and hook kick reps

Hook kick and knife set 8: Hook kick and reverse grip reps

### Basic exercise series 5: Frontal kicks and knife work

Follow the above pattern, and insert a frontal kick.

### Basic exercise series 6: Side kicks and knife work

Follow the above pattern, and insert a side kick.

### Basic exercise series 7: Faking hand motion with knife work

Follow the above pattern, and insert a hand fake.

### Basic exercise series 8: Faking kick motion with knife work

Follow the above pattern, and insert a kicking fake.

### Basic exercise series...

Continue constructing the infinite numbers of combinations.

These should include combinations of three, then four, and so on.

Use all these techniques in the sparring described in Chapter 18.

# Chapter 14

# Grips, Releases and Counters

### Strategy and Drill 1: Introduction to the Trapping and Grappling Ranges

We have proceeded in this encyclopedia thus far from mentality, to stance, to grip, to attacking and blocking, and disarming drills. Now, we will take one step closer to the opponent and deal with the next ranges of combat, the trapping and grappling ranges. This chapter will cover techniques and drills used when you grab the opponent, and with the opponent seizing you.

### 1) The seizures

In the trapping range, the opponent can seize your limbs:

    a)  with a palm-in grip,
    b)  with a palm-out grip,
    c)  with a right hand,
    d)  with a left hand,
    e)  with both hands.

In the trapping and grappling range, the opponent can seize your body:

    a)  with wrapping arms,
    b)  with wrapping legs,

c) with a combination of arms and legs,

d) while one or both of you are standing, kneeling or on the ground.

## 2) The basic counter responses

a) Distractions (fakes, handstrikes, kicks, yelling, pushing, pulling, spitting, etc.),

b) Circular patterns,

c) Push/pull counter forces,

d) Blade attacks,

e) Switching weapon hands counter,

f) Explosive retraction,

g) Impact strikes.

All these techniques will be demonstrated in Hock's knife fighting video series.

With a little maneuvering, Hock could lock his elbows, utilize his body weight and plunge that knife into his opponent's throat.

## Strategy and Drill 2: Grabbing the Knife Hand/Wrist Drills

You must have muscle memory reflex in grabbing the attacker's weapon-bearing limb, whether you are armed or unarmed. Using the Presas 12 angles of attack drill, the angles of which have been detailed several times prior in this encyclopedia, a trainer will feed a trainee the 12 angles. These drills are designed to develop the trainee's grabbing skills.

The trainee will:

### 1) Double-hand grab series

a)  Grab the knife hand/wrist/forearm with both hands. In this first series, then let go so that the flow of the training drill can continue.

b)  In the next series, double-hand grab, and execute any kick. Then let go so you and your partner can continue the drill.

c)  In the next series, double-hand grab, kick, and execute any throw off of the 12 angles of attack. This may well be one of the most important drills in this encyclopedia. Practice it often and wisely. Here is a sample of a double-handed catch off of an attack angle.

### 2) Single-hand grab series

You are armed with a knife vs. the 12 angles:

a)  Grab the trainer's knife hand/wrist/ forearm with your free backup hand (then release so the flow of the drill can continue).

b)  Grab the trainer's knife hand/wrist/ forearm with your free backup hand, then slash the trainer with your knife in a saber grip. You may designate any target through a whole series of 12 or change them.

Typical targets for the knife in this drill are:

1) hand,
2) wrist,
3) forearm,
4) bicep,
5) throat.

c) Grab the trainer's knife hand/wrist/forearm with your free backup hand, then with your knife in a reverse grip, stab the trainer.

Familiarize yourself with these drills. Not only do they build great self-defense skills, but also they are required knowledge when you practice the upcoming counters.

## Strategy and Drill 3: Circular Pattern Releases

Circular pattern releases can run clockwise or counter-clockwise. The important things to remember about these circles are, that if you violently rotate your captured hand in these directions, you should have a successful release from your opponent's grip, so do not hesitate or ponder which direction you should choose. Just start circling! Secondly, if you are freeing your knife hand, your blade might assist the release by cutting the opponent's gripping limb. Your backup hand also can assist in the knife hand's escape by pushing or pulling.

The first two are circular releases. The second pair are half-circles and stabs.

### 1) The clockwise release

Your weapon-bearing wrist has been grabbed. Distract by spitting, shouting, kicking, whatever means you find appropriate. Then, whether you hold your knife in a saber or icepick grip, draw your knife hand, or your captured backup hand in a tight circular, clockwise pattern until your opponent loses the majority of his grip tension.

Clockwise release of empty hands

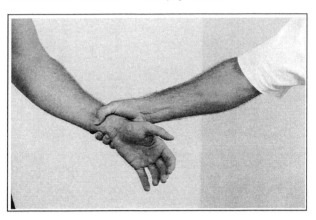

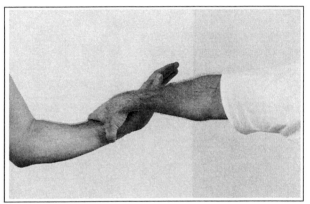

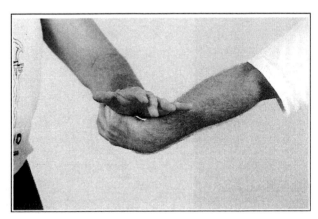

Clockwise release from saber grip

Clockwise release from reverse grip

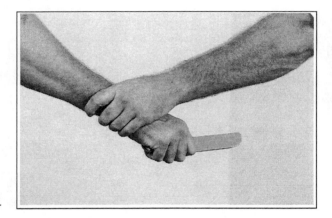

1

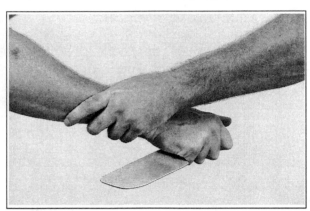

1

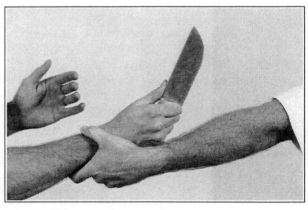

2

2

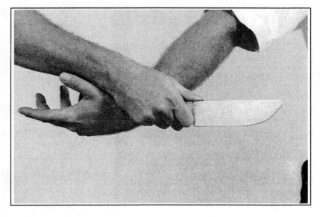

3

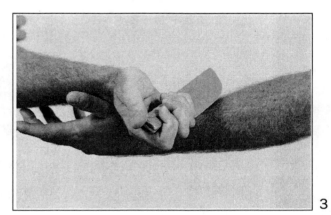

3

Clockwise release from a two-handed grip

Counter-clockwise release of the backup hand

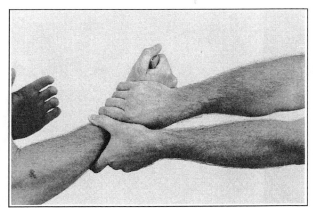

1

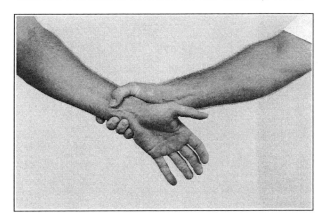

1

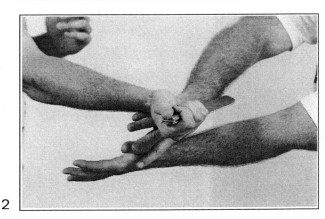

2

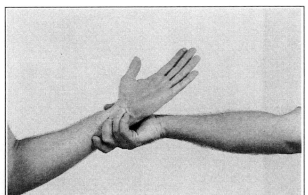

2

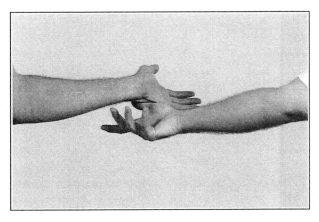

3

## 2) The counter-clockwise release

Your weapon-bearing wrist has been grabbed. Distract by spitting, shouting, kicking, whatever means you find appropriate. Then, whether you hold your knife in a saber or icepick grip, draw your knife hand, or captured backup hand, in a tight counter clockwise circular pattern until your opponent loses his grip tension.

Counter-clockwise saber grip release

Counter-clockwise reverse grip release

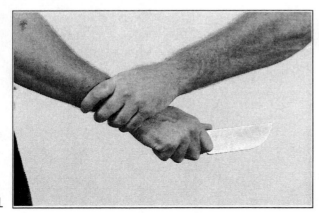

1

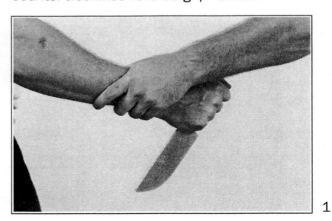

1

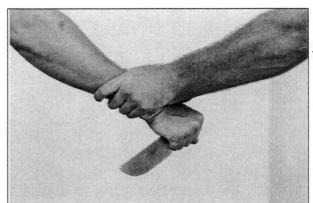

2

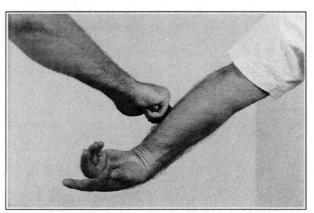

2

3

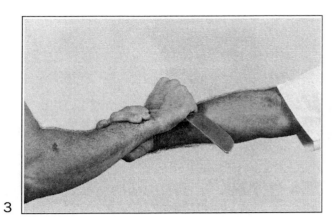

3

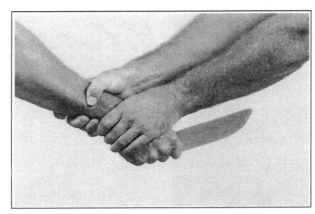

4

Counter-clockwise release from a two-handed capture

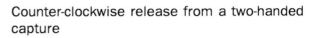

1

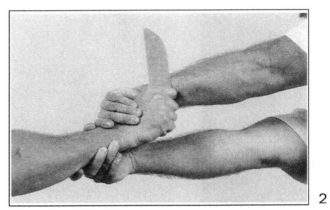

2

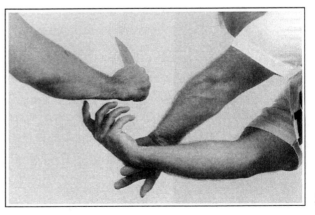

3

### 3) Groin stab

The opponent grips your weapon-bearing right wrist with his left hand, palm-down.

You make a circle with your knife hand in front of the opponent, and stab the opponent's groin. You may or may not choose to use your left hand on the opponent's upper arm to help facilitate the movement with a pin or a push.

### 4) Chest stab

The opponent grips your weapon-bearing right wrist with his left hand, palms-down.

You make a small, clockwise, half-circle, winding the knife upward and beside the outside of the opponent's wrist. If the opponent's grip is tight enough, this will place his forearm and upper arm in an awkward position, almost an "S" or "V" lock position. Using forward pressure, drive the blade into the upper chest or throat. You may or may not choose to use your left hand upon the opponent's elbow to facilitate the movement with a pin or push.

**Advanced circular pattern drill training**
This is the counter to the drills in the previous section. Using the Presas 12 angles of attack, you slash at the opponent. The opponent seizes your weapon-bearing wrist. You immediately execute a circular release, and free yourself. Then re-attack with the next angle in the drill. This is great practice!

## Strategy and Drill 4: The Push/Pull Pattern Releases

These releases work off of an impact on the seizing limb with an assisting yank free of your knife hand.

### 1) Victimized by a palm-in grip

Your opponent holds your knife-bearing wrist or forearm with a palm-in grip. Distract by shouting, spitting, kicking, whatever means you find appropriate. Then you slap the opponent's forearm outward as you pull your knife hand inward through the opening between his fingers and his palm.

Push/pull counter of a saber grip

Push/pull counter with empty hands

Push/pull counter release of a reverse grip

## 2) Victimized by a palm-out grip

Your opponent holds your knife-bearing wrist with a palm-outward grip. Distract by shouting, spitting, kicking, whatever means you find appropriate. Then you grab his gripping forearm, and pull it away from your seized limb, as you push your knife hand away from the grip.

Empty-handed counter

Saber grip counter

Reverse grip counter

1

1

2

2

## 3) Advanced push-pull release training drill

This is another counter drill vs. the Presas 12 angles of attack. You attack. Your trainer grabs your weapon-bearing limb. You push/pull a release, then continue the attack with the next angle. This is great practice. Below are some sample photos of an angle 1 attack.

1

3

2

4

## Strategy and Drill 5: Blade Stab Releases

If your weapon hand or backup hand is seized, you can often use your knife tip to assist in an escape.

### 1) Stab or cut the seizing forearm

Distract by spitting, shouting, striking, whatever means you find appropriate. Inject the blade into the gripping forearm. Carry this motion violently through into a release.

Saber grip attack vs. a grip of the backup hand

Reverse grip attack vs. grip on backup hand

Reverse grip attack on same hand

## 2) Stab or cut the arm or torso

If you are holding a knife in a saber grip and your opponent seizes your forearm with either hand:

a) strike the opponent's forearm or biceps to weaken the strength in the arm,

b) using all your body strength, stab the blade forward into the torso.

Counter the right-handed grip with a strike to the right gripping limb.

Counter the left-handed grip with a strike to the forearm or biceps.

1

1

2

2

3

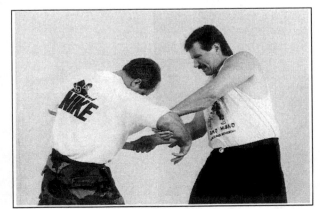

3

Counter the gripping left hand on your backup hand with a knife attack.

**3) Practice these releases from the 12 angles of attack**

# Strategy and Drill 6: The Even-Even Grip Releases

Remember in many of the old westerns, there were scenes where the cowboy faced off the Indian in a climatic battle? Each armed, the pair often wrestled to a dramatic standstill, the cowboy's backup hand gripped the Indian's knife hand/wrist tightly, the Indian vice-versa. Pushing strength vs. pushing strength with dramatic gasping, sweat and teeth-clinching. A little re-direction of that energy might have gone a long way, and does in a real-life fight.

In these armed sometimes called "Even-Indian" or "Even-Steven" releases, each partner is holding the other's weapon-bearing wrist, and one will train to win their release out of a grappling struggle. He who first lets lose of the opponent's knife wrist, will mostly likely get injured by that knife.

Distracting the opponent at the point of action is important. Again, yelling, spitting, kicks or knees to the groin or the rest of the body help facilitate release.

Two goals:

1) Use the knife as a tool to release the opponent's grip on your knife arm, or
2) Use the knife as a tool to release the opponent's grip on your backup hand.

## 1) The three saber grip "even-even" releases

1) Slash or saw the opponent's knife forearm
2) Circular release
3) Push/pull, trap and stab

### Release 1: The slash

Experience the push and pull between your knife hand and the resistance your opponent is giving you. Based upon your estimation of the push/pull energy between you, estimate when you can best force your hands together in a clapping like motion. Distract. Then bring your hands together and try to slash the opponent's weapon-bearing arm. Cut the opponent's weapon-bearing forearm with your blade.

Work it in a sawing motion, if possible. If you are superior in strength to this opponent, you might be able to actually maneuver yourself into sawing the knife hand of the opponent!

With the opponent's resulting weakness and shock, spring quickly and attack.

## Release 2: Circular releases

Twist your knife-bearing wrist in a clockwise or counter-clockwise direction and snake around your opponent's grip. Try to force this into a release for your knife hand.

1

2

3

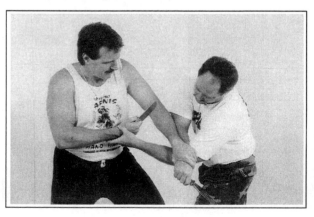

4

1

2

3

### Release 3: The push/pull, trap and stab

Try to experience the push/pull energy between you and your opponent.

### Downward impact trapping

If you notice your opponent's weapon hand has a side-to-side give to it, with a significant distraction, sidestep and try to smash his knife hand down atop his free hand forearm, the hand holding your knife-bearing wrist. If you are lucky, or if you are strong enough to control the path, his knife-tip will hit his own forearm.

While you are doing this, turn your knife hand palm upward. As this trapping impact hits his forearm, try to pull your knife hand upward and free, in the direction of the opening in his grip.

You might get a cut on his arm during this push/pull. Immediately stab at his throat while this trap is temporarily in place, because as in all trapping in the martial arts, the trap is only in place for a micro-second.

4

If he has a reverse grip on his knife, try to momentarily catch his backup forearm between the knife-bearing forearm and the blade of his own knife.

## Upward impact trapping

Or, you can trap with an upward impact. From an Even-Steven grip, after a significant distraction, force the opponent's knife hand downward and inside. Try to get him to slash his own opposite forearm. If his knife cuts his own forearm, or even if it misses, let the momentum continue, allowing his knife hand to drop lower than your knife hand's height. At this point, he should be exerting some reverse energy resistance. Take advantage of this. Turn your knife hand palm down, so that the opening in the opponent's hand is also facing downward. Then, using your free hand wrist and/or forearm along with his captured knife hand wrist and/or forearm, blast upward through his grip. This should release his grip upon your weapon-bearing

limb in the classic push/pull fashion. Stab the torso. Continue with any appropriate follow-ups.

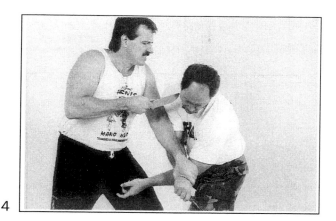

1

2

3

4

5

## 2) The 3 reverse grip releases
1) Icepick stab
2) Crook hook
3) Grab stab

**Reverse grip release 1: The icepick stab**

There are two ways to use this icepick stab:

a) stab the arm that is holding your knife, or

b) stab the arm that is holding your back-up hand.

### Stab a) Stab the arm that holds your knife

You feel the push/pull and side-by-side hand energy with your opponent. When the energy is appropriate, bury the tip of your knife into the forearm or bicep of the enemy.

## Stab b) Stab the arm that holds your weapon bearing limb

The purpose of this exercise is to stab the tip of the blade into the forearm of the opponent's arm that is gripping your weapon-bearing hand.

1) rotate your wrist into a position where you can do this. Success depends largely upon how high or low the grip is on your forearm.
2) with "forward punch" energy, spring your knife hand forward, then yank downward with a stab to the forearm.

## Reverse grip release 2: The crook hook

For this situation, for this crook hook to work, instead of having a palm-inward grip on your opponent's knife bearing wrist, you must have a palm-outward grip.

You feel the push/pull and side-by-side hand energy with your opponent. When the energy is appropriate, distract. Over the top of the arm, hook your knife in the bend

of your opponent's arm, the so-called "crook" of the arm. If possible, try to turn the edge of the knife into the bend to cut the arm.

Pull/cut inward toward his center at first. With your grip upon his knife bearing wrist, push downward and back as you pull your hooking knife inward. Step to the side. This is a lever-action takedown. Use low line kicks to the knee, if needed. Use the impact, or a kick or a circular release to free your knife hand.

1

2

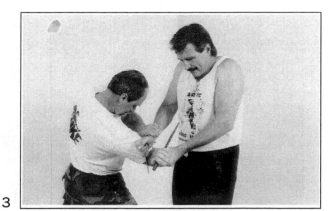

3

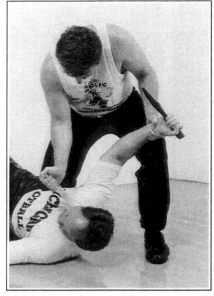

6

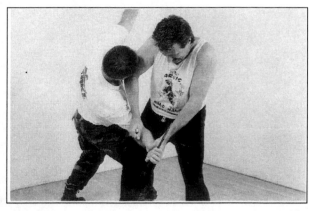

4

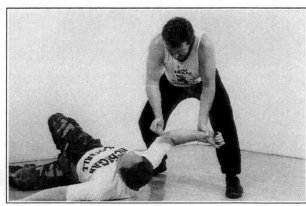

5

If the opponent is holding his knife in a reverse grip also, you might disarm his knife by wedging it out with your forearm. Shown in the Disarm chapter. See the reverse grip strip disarm.

### Reverse grip release 3: Grab and stab

In this situation, when the energy is appropriate, distract, then try to bring the opponent's weapon-bearing forearm down upon his other forearm, the one gripping you. If you are lucky, if you are strong enough, you may steer his own knife tip to pierce this forearm.

If this forearm lands atop his gripping forearm, try to use this as a "trap," immobilizing his gripping hand. Yank your knife hand free under this trap, and stab the throat. You might continue with a blade to blade push/pull disarm and strip the knife.

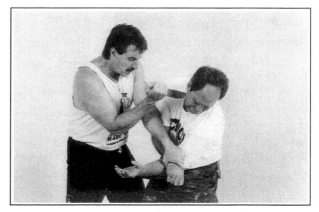

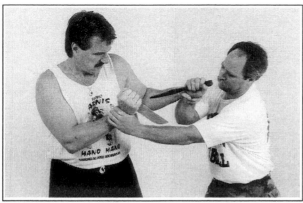

**The shoulder "loop" release**

If both fighters are facing each other and holding each other's weapon-bearing wrists in the "Even-Even" grip. Each hold their knives in the saber grip. To successfully execute the release:

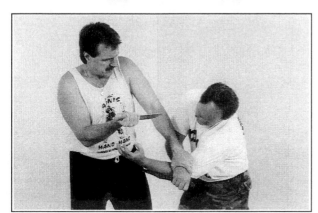

a) you execute a head butt to the nose of the opponent,

b) you pin the knife hand you are gripping, tight up against the opponent's side,

c) you step under the arm that is holding your knife hand, looping the opponent's arm over your shoulder,

d) using your whole torso and leg power, push up against the arm on your back, and down on your knife hand. This should free your knife hand from the opponent's grip.

e) Attack the opponent. Either immediately stab the opponent, or slash the tendons of the opponent's weapon-bearing arm, and then stab or slash a vital target. The option will depend on whether you need to defang the blade first, or not.

1

2

3

4

5

6

# Chapter 15

# Chain of the Knife Drills

## Introduction to the Chain Drills

Another training regimen to improve specific knife fighting techniques is through chain drills. This term comes from the Filipino Cadena De Mano or "chain of the hand." It refers to the flowing and linking of techniques. In this regard, it would be called Cadena De Daga, or "chain of the knife." These drills also resemble Chinese Wing Chun Gung Fu, "dummy" drills. The drills can introduce new techniques, be prescribed to trouble shoot performance deficiencies, develop the flow or just hone skills.

The chain drill can offer specific, ambidextrous development, as the practitioner can work both left and right sides, inside and outside responses. Work both left and right knife hands. Then experiment with a double knife approach.

There are two training versions of the chain drill, one still-sometimes called "statue" drills, and one in limited motion. Start with the stationary drill to establish the specifics of the technique, then advance to the motion drill. Either way, the trainer may choose to hold a knife in each hand, either hand or be empty handed. The practice should include work with both a saber or reverse grip.

1) Stationary. In the stationary drill, the trainer will stand with both of his arms out and shoulder width apart before the practitioner. Depending upon the techniques practiced in the drill, the trainer may keep his arms and hands shoulder height, or bent at the waist, or may switch during the progression.

2) Motion. In the motion drill, the trainer will feed the attack to give a more realistic feel to the practice. This looks like pistons firing. It is still controlled to allow the practitioner time to develop.

1

2

3

4

# Chain Drill 1: Torso Stab

This drill develops the basic slap and mid-section stab. It is described from a right-handed perspective. Just switch hands for left-handed training.

**The stationary drill**

The trainer will hold his arms high and shoulder width apart.

2

**Step 1:** With a left hand, the practitioner slaps the hand/wrist area inward and stabs the right, torso area of the trainer, usually with a palm up, horizontal blade stab.

**Step 2:** With a left-handed backhand on the opponent's right arm, the practitioner stabs the torso.

**Step 3:** With a left hand, the practitioner slaps the hand/wrist area of the trainer's left arm outward, then stabs the torso.

**Step 4:** With a left-handed backhand upon the trainer's left arm, the practitioner stabs the outer side torso of the trainer, usually with a palm down stab.

3

4

**Motion drill**

Repeat the same steps as above, only the trainer will feed his arms in for the response. As the trainer's speed increases, the play can become quite lively!

1

# Chain Drill 2: The Upper Arm Destruction

This Cadena De Daga drill develops destruction slashing muscle memory.

**The Stationary drill version**

In this drill, there are four "links"—two high and two low. This means that the trainer must offer the practitioner four targets. The trainer starts with two high arms, then when the practitioner is through with the high series, the trainer lowers his arms to bend them at the waist for that series.

**Step 1:** The practitioner slaps the hand/wrist area inward with the left palm, then slashes the tricep of the right arm.

**Step 2:** Reverse this action. The practitioner backhands the hand/wrist area and slashes the right tricep.

**Step 3:** The practitioner slaps the hand/wrist area outward with a left palm, then slashes the tricep of the right arm.

**Step 4:** Reverse this action. The practitioner backhands the hand/wrist area and slashes the left tricep.

The trainer lowers his arms, bending them.

**Step 5:** The practitioner slaps the hand wrist area inward with the left palm, then slashes the bicep of the right arm.

**Step 6:** Reverse this action. The practitioner backhands the hand/wrist area and slashes the right bicep.

**Step 7:** The practitioner slaps the hand/wrist outward with a left palm, then slashes the left bicep.

**Step 8:** Reverse this action. The practitioner backhands the hand/wrist area and slashes the left bicep.

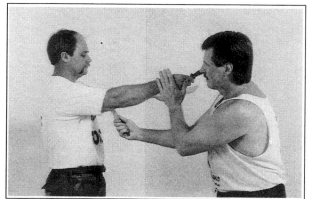

1

2

3

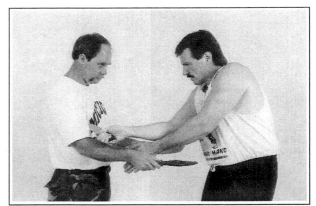

6

4

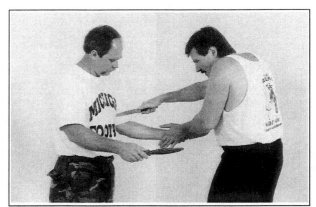

7

5

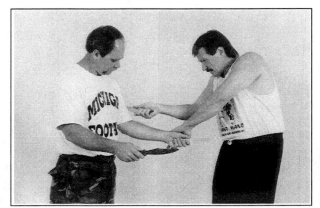

8

## Freestyle variations

In no fixed pattern, take these skills to the next level by feeding a host of quick angles. Add two kicks into the pattern, and have the practitioner slash the thighs.

## Chain Drill 3: Thigh Slash

This drill develops the basic thigh slash. It is described from a right-handed perspective. Just switch hands for left-handed training.

**The stationary drill**

The trainer will hold his arms high and shoulder width apart.

**Step 1:** With his left hand, the practitioner slaps the hand/wrist area inward, and slashes the right thigh of the trainer, usually with a palm up, horizontal blade stab.

**Step 2:** With a left-handed backhand on the opponent's right arm, the practitioner slashes the right thigh of the trainer, usually with the palm down.

**Step 3:** With a left hand, the practitioner slaps the hand/wrist area of the trainer's left arm outward, then slashes the left torso.

**Step 4:** With a left-handed backhand upon the trainer's left arm, the practitioner slashes the left thigh of the trainer.

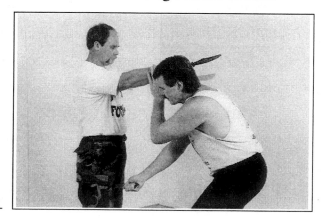

1

2

3

4

**Motion drill**

Repeat the same steps as above, only the trainer will feed his arms in for the response.

## Chain Drill 4: Scoop the Knee

This drill develops the use of a knife in a takedown progression. In this drill, the trainer may position his arms high or mid-range, because the target areas are behind the knee and the front of the throat. Think about putting the sharp edge of the blade against the leg or throat, if you are working with a single-edged knife. Each step of this drill should only initiate a takedown, so you can continue the practice.

**Step 1:** The practitioner steps to the right side, outside, places the left palm on the chin and pushes as the blade works behind the knee and lifts.

**Step 2:** The practitioner steps to the inside and places the blade up against the throat, and scoops the knee with the left hand.

**Step 3:** The practitioner steps to the inside and places the left palm on the chin and pushes as the blade works behind the knee and lifts.

**Step 4:** The practitioner steps to the left side, outside, places the blade up against the throat, and scoops the knee with the left hand.

In the first photo, top left, I am reaching around to Tom Barnhart's neck and chin from the outside of his arms. This "outside" approach is preferable to some practitioners. In the other photos, my arm attacks on the inside. Remember that the chain drills are just that, "drills!" They open up your line of familiarization and build muscle memory.

1

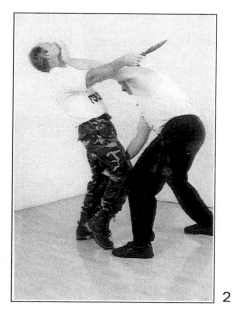

2

3

4

## Chain Drill 5: Finger Slash

This drill develops the basic hand slash. It is described from a right-handed perspective. Just switch hands for left-handed training. Work with a saber and reverse grip.

**The stationary drill**
The trainer will hold his arms high and shoulder width apart.

**Step 1:** The practitioner slashes the weapon-bearing right hand fingers on an inward 45-degree angle slash (angle 1).

**Step 2:** The practitioner slashes the weapon-bearing right hand fingers in a back-handed manner, on a 45-degree angle (angle 2).

**Step 3:** The practitioner slashes the weapon-bearing left hand fingers in an inward manner.

**Step 4:** The practitioner slashes the weapon-bearing left hand fingers in a back-handed manner.

**Motion drill**
Repeat the same steps as above, only the trainer will feed his arms in for the response.

## Summary

These chain drills isolate techniques and develop the flow every knife-fighter needs. The drills dissected in this chapter are very basic. You must develop similar drills as you need them for your training. Use them as a prescription to problem-solving. Remember these fundamentals when you do.

The trainer in these chain drills offers:

a)  statue or stationary training,
b)  motion training,
c)  either holds one or more knives, or can be empty handed.

The trainee should:

a)  practice with the knife in the right hand,
b)  practice with the knife in the left hand,
c)  practice with two knives, if possible, within the drill.

Hock and V.P. Tom Barnhart oversee a ground fighting scenario at an annual Knife Fighter Summit in Dallas, Texas.

# Chapter 16

# Skill Developing Drills

## Introduction

So often I read knife training manuals and watch knife training videos, and their simplicity of what they teach and show, amazes me. Rarely do they demonstrate methods and explanations beyond "this is a slash," or "this is a stab" type instruction. There is no talk of the flow, no structure or means to pass the flow onto their students.

Like catching a ground ball in baseball, running a pass pattern in football, or practicing a golf swing, there are a multitude of things that can be done to perfect the minutest parts of a single athletic act, therefore enhancing skill.

The drills in this chapter are skill developing drills, many from the Filipino Martial Arts, that work muscle memory like a professional athlete.

You will probably never master these drills by reading this chapter. They need to be demonstrated, as they are in my knife videos, and they require hands-on practice with an experienced partner.

# Filipino Hubod

"What is that? Teach me that!" Martial artists from coast to coast, black belt to white, upon seeing "hubod," plead to learn this close-quarter drill with hundreds of knife, stick and empty hand variations. Basic hubod is one of the most versatile, skill-developing drills a martial artist can find. The drill simulates that first instant of a clinch, when two opponents go elbow to elbow.

Filipino hubod is a sensitivity drill that involves three steps per partner, making the revolution of the drill between two partners a total of six counts, or beats. It can be practiced standing, kneeling, on the ground, or any combination thereof.

Any strike, kick, push, pull, lock, disarm or throw can be achieved inside the hubod drill by changing the response on a particular beat, or inserting a half-beat technique. Half-beat training causes you to fire an attack on the half-second in amidst this flow.

Some of my instructors demanded hubod be done very lightly and soft. Others have instructed me the opposite. Hard! Do hubod with JKD Concepts instructor Paul Vunak, and you'll walk away with your arms feeling as though you were wrestling a bear! Yet, I tested in another American/Kali system and in a rank test, the instructor rated me poorly in hubod! I asked why, and he said I was doing it, "too

hard. Hubod should be soft!" he declared.

So, some will teach it soft or hard, with wide and high grandiose motions. A few will insist on keeping the transaction close and contained tightly to the small of the chest area. After all these differing exposures, I think it would be best to work hubod soft and hard, as well as grandiose and tight. Do all four for variety. But do it! It is enlightening! Just don't let anyone say you are wrong to practice it one way or the other.

Hubod is traditionally meant to flow. This is difficult sometimes when, for one example, you are achieving a knife lock because if you successfully complete the knife lock, your partner cannot continue with the flow of the drill! Therefore, sometimes a practitioner will not complete the lock, but rather get the feel of its cementing, or the beginning of its success. Then the practitioner will release the partner to continue the flow of the drill. The other option is to break the flow and get the strike, lock, or throw completed. Then you start up the drill with a fresh attack at the selected angle.

## Basic knife hubod drills

It would take another entire encyclopedia to describe the multitude of inserts because hubod can be used to embrace virtually every close quarter fighting technique. I can only present some basic drills and samples of each in this encyclopedia. The samples should help you fill in the gaps. Please pay specific attention to the dissection of the movements by beat. Like musical beats in a song, they will help set the pace of the drill and technique. There will be actions on half and even quarter beats! You can and should add more of your own follow-ups.

## Drill 1: The six-count saber grip hubod drill

Most commonly taught hubod starts with the right hand "chopping" down upon the left side of the partner's neck, as the first beat. In terms of our knife fighting practice, this becomes a slash or a reverse-knife-grip stab to the throat.

**Step 1:** With his right hand, your partner attacks at a 45-degree angle downward to slash the left side of your throat. You block with your left forearm to his right forearm.

**Step 2:** Your right hand, which is your knife-hand, goes under his forearm and in a clockwise manner you sweep down and away from the attack. For the purpose of this drill, the opponent's attacking arm should have a bend in it. The attacking arm is swept down in front of you, about solar plexus high.

**Step 3:** You pin the partner's elbow area with the palm of your left hand.

**Step 4:** Holding this elbow pin, now you attack the left side of your partner's neck. He in turn blocks with his left forearm.

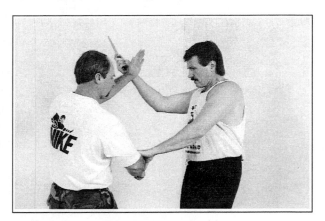

**Step 5:** Your partner now sweeps his right hand up under your right forearm. You do not release pressure on the partner's right elbow until you are convinced that his arm is moving to do this sweep.

**Step 6:** With the palm of his left hand, the partner pins your right elbow, about solar plexus high.

You continue the flow...

## Drill 2: The six-count reverse grip hubod drill

Repeat the same steps except hold the knife in a reverse grip. The attacks become stabs not slashes.

1

4

2

5

3

6

### Drill 3: Four corner saber hubod

Uncommonly taught or practiced, few know that hubod can actually be initiated from the four corners of the window of combat, and this makes for a good practice drill. Briefly:

**Angle 1:** This angle is as detailed in the first two drills. High right hand attack, your left arm blocks high, right crosses, both sweep down, then your partner attacks at the original angle. You respond with your half of the drill.

**Angle 2:** High left hand attack, your right arm blocks high, left crosses, both sweep down, then your partner attacks at the original angle. You respond with the drill.

3

4

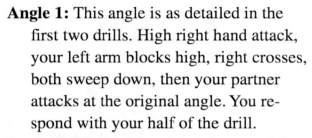

1

5

2

6

**Angle 3:** Low right attack, your left arm
blocks low, right crosses, both sweep
aside, then your partner attacks at the
original angle. You respond with the
drill.

1

4

2

5

3

6

**Angle 4:** Low left hand attack, your right arm blocks low, left crosses, both sweep aside, then your partner attacks at the original angle. You will respond with the drill.

1

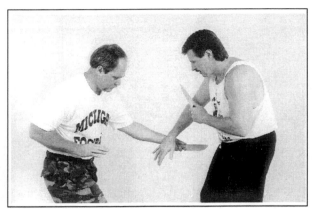

4

2

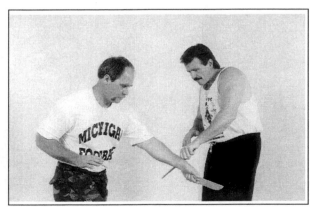

5

3

6

**Drill 4: The half-beat saber slash drill**

Slash either the weapon bearing arm, or if possible, the throat of the opponent, on every half-beat of the six-count drill. This will involve trapping hands and grappling manipulations. Mastering this drill will bring you incredible, close-quarter, knife fighting savvy, with skill development in:

1) Defanging the Snake, weapon-bearing hand and wrist cuts,
2) basic destructions to the secondary body part targets,
3) killshot slashes.

Here are two sample half-beat slashes:

a) **Slash on beat 1 1/2**

**Beat 1:** You block the incoming attack with your left forearm.

**Beat 1 1/2:** Instead of taking your right knife-hand under the attacking arm to execute the block, you simply slash the inside of the opponent's arm with your knife hand, and slash or stab immediately to his throat. The photo series shows me slashing Tom Barnhart's wrist, but you can substitute higher targets on the half-beat.

## b: Throat slash on beat 3 1/2

**Beats 1, 2, 3:** Execute the pattern as normal.

**Beat 3 1/2:** You can reach for the head hair of the opponent, usually on the rear of the head, and slash the throat. Or, as in the photo series, if you feel the need to keep the opponent's knife-hand pinned, keep your backup hand there.

1

3

2

4

## c) Slash on beat 6 1/2

**Beats 1, 2, 3, 4, 5, 6:** Execute the pattern as normal.

**Beat 6 1/2:** As the opponent's hand pushes down on your weapon-bearing elbow area for a pin, grab his wrist with your freehand and pull it up, while lowering your knife-hand. Once your knife-hand is free, slash the stomach.

1

2

3

4

## Drill 5: The half-beat slash reverse grip drill

Simply repeat the same basic steps as described in the half-beat slash drill, utilizing a stab or reverse grip slash instead of a saber slash. Practice attacks on the half-beat.

## Drill 6: The switching hands and attack on half-beat drill

On the half-beats, try to switch hands and stab or slash at any available target. Experiment with either grip.

## Drill 7: Miscellaneous fighting techniques out of hubod

Use these specific parts of hubod drills to inspire your practice and growth. I have purposely not chosen techniques that appear in other techniques in the encyclopedia to prevent redundancy. Just remember, you can break down almost every close-quarter fighting technique and train in through the high-speed flow of hubod.

a) Attempt a snake disarm of your partner's reverse grip on beat 1 1/2. Wedge your forearm between the blade and his forearm. Use your forearm against the flat of the blade, and twist it out.

This technique is categorized in the Disarm Chapter.

b) Attempt an armbar hammerlock, or a rear armbar on beat 2 1/2. Get to bargaining position with a knife to the throat. Make sure your single edge blade is turned in toward the throat. Remember that there are many nuisances to the rear armbar or armbar hammerlock. Training and developing this armbar could be the subject of a small book or a whole video in itself.

4

1

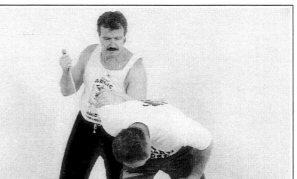

5

2

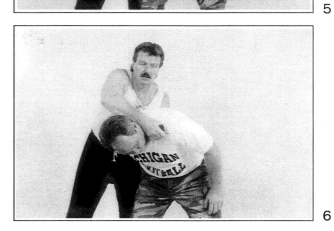

6

3

7

265

c) With your reverse grip, attempt an underarm leverlock takedown on beat 1 1/2 by inserting your knife bearing arm under the tricep area of the partner, by weaving the blade of the knife under the tricep and on top of the partner's wrist. You may need the flat surface of the blade to exert enough force to lever action the forearm into a takedown. Insert a behind the knee kick if needed.

d) Attempt any low-line kick on any half-beat.

e) Experiment to see if any martial arts technique will flow.

All these hubod techniques and more are demonstrated and explained in Hock's Hubod Knife Fighting video. Remember to experiment in all four corners of the drill.

1

3

2

4

## Torso Attack

The torso attack drill is a give and take, knife vs. knife drill, which develops skills in close-quarter fighting stabbing, cutting, and blocking. Later, knife disarms can be worked in the drill. It has 4 angles of stabbing attacks. The trainer holds his knife in the "saber" position and stabs. The trainee holds the blade in a reverse or icepick grip.

**The trainer's angles of attack are:**

1) high to the trainee's left shoulder area (knuckles inward)
2) high to the trainee's right shoulder area (knuckles outward)
3) low to the trainee's left side of the stomach area (knuckles outward)
4) low to the trainee's right side of the stomach area. (knuckles outward)

1, 2

3

4

## The trainee's responses vs. angles 1-4

1) On each of the 4 angles follow this pattern:

   a) cut the attacking limb,

   b) grab the attacking limb,

   c) return a stab to the throat.

It becomes the trainer's job to block the trainee's stab to the throat, with a hand to your attacking wrist. Then the trainer continues the attack drill with the next angle. Here my friend and training partner Tom Barnhart works through the drill.

Angle 1 attack

3

4

1

5

2

6

Angle 2 attack

Angle 3 attack

1

1

2

2

3

3

Angle 4 attack

1

2

**Some advanced practice follow-ups**

1) Off angle 1, twist the captured arm elbow down, hook the blade in the bend of the arm, lever down on the wrist, lever up in the bend.

1

2

3

4

3

2) Off angle 2, acquire a figure four lock/ takedown. Cut the throat on the way.

1

4

2

5

6

7

3) Off angle 3, catch the wrist area, and jam your blade into the crook of the arm. Shove the trainer's knife into his side.

1

2

3

4

4) Advanced double stab off of angle 3, grab the weapon-bearing wrist. Jam your blade into the crook of the arm, then move your knife hand down the forearm, turning the blade toward the body. End up with the pummel on the trainer's wrist. Now you have two blades pointing at the opponent's side. Shove both blades into his side.

Some Filipino practitioners enjoy a push/pull maneuver before the stabbing. They pull out and downward causing the opponent's body to fall into the blades while the blades are then pushed into the torso. Some also enjoy foot trapping at this point — that is stepping on the opponent's foot to keep it from moving — for balance.

5) Off angle 4: Use the blade to catch and bend the trainer's weapon-bearing arm, then execute a rear armbar hammerlock, getting the opponent into bargaining position.

6) And more... Make up your own responses. Remember, the more exotic, the less likely they will work in a real fight.

## Knife Sumbrada

In the Philippines, it is often remarked that an Arnisador trains his or her whole life for a four-second stick fight, and the same is true for knife fighting combatants.

One phenomenal drill to prepare yourself for such life and death encounters is something called Sumbrada in the Filipino Martial Arts. The Filipino word or term Sumbrada has multiple meanings, just like many of our words do in the English language. In Philippine Tagalog, Sumbrada loosely translates to "shadow-boxing," and also has become a universal training term found throughout the varied systems of Arnis/Kali/Escrima. Sumbrada drills usually refer to a close-quarter range of combat. With the stick or knife, it usually means a range where the tip of the weapon can reach the partner's head, and your backup hand can touch the partner's weapon-bearing hand.

Sumbrada has now, through American/Filipino evolution come to mean specific and identifiable drills. The differences between the drills may only be the amounts of strikes and blocks involved, or the patterns exercised.

But as this writing will articulate, Sumbrada training is not exclusively knife-related! The basic drills also include practice in:

1) sword and hand vs. sword and hand
2) double sword vs. double sword
3) double stick vs. double stick
4) knife and stick vs. knife and stick
5) knife and hand vs. knife and hand
6) double knives vs. double knives
7) hand-to-hand
8) weapon combinations, such as double stick vs. stick and knife, etc.

If Arnisadors can successfully practice Sumbrada in each of these categories, they are accomplishing a comprehensive achievement in the Filipino Martial Arts.

Basic and advanced studies in Sumbrada drill will develop mental and muscle memory in:

1) blocking
2) striking
3) rapid fire counter-attacking
4) footwork
5) peripheral vision
6) strength and endurance
7) coordination
8) courage to go close-up and face-to-face
9) hand trapping
10) stick catching
11) disarming

The drill I have selected to explain in this encyclopedia is a basic 10-step single knife Sumbrada drill. There are shorter versions, but none quite as comprehensive as this one. The knife is in the primary hand, and the empty hand is the support hand. You must keep your checking/trapping hand on the opponent's free hand as you begin your return strike. Let loose of this "drag" upon the opponent's hand when you are convinced that the only place it will travel is to support his block.

There are 10 beats or "events." By events, I mean 10 strikes and blocks or 10 impacts. They occur in what is often called the box pattern, but it is actually more like a horseshoe shape around the top and sides of the practitioners.

Here is a brief overview of the five strikes and five blocks of 10-count Sumbrada.

## Five basic blockings
1) Umbrella block the hirada, knife tip horizontal or down

2) Drop block, knife tip up

3) Shield block, knife tip down

4) Cross the body block, right-handed knife to the left side block, knife tip up

5) Cross body block, right-handed knife right side block) knife tip down

**Five basic strikings**
1) Strike to the right side of the head or neck

2) Strike to the right side of the torso (can substitute a torso stab here)

3) Overhead strike

4) Strike to the left side of the head

5) Strike to the left side of the torso

Try to remember or say out loud as you practice the chant of "block, strike, block, strike, block, strike..." This is exactly what you are doing. To start, the practitioners must stand before each other in close range, face-to-face. Designate who will begin the drill, usually starting with a high right slash to the left side of the partner's neck or head.

## "A" is one person, "B" is the other.

**Beat 1:** A) Strike to the left head area...
B) Umbrella block

**Beat 2:** B) Strike to the left head area...
A) Cross body block

**Beat 3:** A) Strike to right torso area...
B) Same side block

**Beat 4:** B) Strike to left torso area...
A) Cross body block (could be a thrust at the torso) tip down

**Beat 5:** A) Fanning wrist flick strike to the right head area...
B) Shield block

**Beat 6:** B) Strike to the left head area...
A) Umbrella block

**Beat 7:** A) Strike to right head area...
B) Cross body block

**Beat 8:** B) Back-hand strike to right...
A) Cross body block torso area

**Beat 9:** A) Strike to left torso...
B) Cross body block (could be a thrust at the torso) tip down

**Beat 10:** B) Fanning wrist flick strike
  to the right head area...
A) Shield block

...and the drill continues again with A's strike to the left side of B's head...

You will never learn the subtleties and proper feel for Sumbrada through reading a book or viewing a tape. You must go up against a qualified instructor. I have been teaching Sumbrada for eight years, and I have honed a lesson plan of gradual development. Step-by-step with a student, I look, and more importantly, feel for many vital points as we practice, adding each new step after completing many flawless repetitions.

Get with a certified instructor to get it right! And also remember, each instructor may have a personal preference on how small things are executed. One of my instructors emphasized the "drag" hand— that is holding your checking hand on the opponent's empty hand to the very last second. Another banged the sticks or knives together as if we were in a medieval sword fight. Another sought out the flow. But through all this, it is most important that you grasp the universal fundamentals to reap the many benefits of Sumbrada.

Now you are ready to insert advanced strategies.

a) Develop your knife hand catching skills at each angle. Remember if you can't catch the enemy's knife hand, you can't do most of the disarms and takedowns.
b) Work a disarm at each angle.
c) Insert a fake at each angle.
d) Execute takedowns.
e) Go as fast and as cleanly as possible.
f) Try freestyling—break the pattern and experiment.

g) Now try these other weapons, use a knife and a stick. Suddenly, you are training Espada Y Daga! Use two sticks. Or two knives. Just remember, when you switch weapons or work empty hands there are certain nuisances that change slightly, but the original jobs of the primary and backup hands remain the same. They perform just as they did in the single stick drill. Unless you purposely switch hands!

Sumbrada offers a developmental ladder and a foundation from which to practice and grow. I hope this peaks your interest in Sumbrada, and the beautiful and deadly art of the Philippines that I have grown to love—Arnis!

## One Attack Statue Drills

In this drill, the trainer attacks the trainee on a freestyle, unplanned angle. The trainee lets muscle memory take over in the response. What makes this drill a progressive skill developer is that:

**Drill 1:** The trainer freezes after he initiates the attack and allows the trainee to practice an elongated attack full of stabs, slashes, etc. anywhere on the body.

**Drill 2:** The trainer reacts in slow-motion after he initiates the attack, and allows the trainee to practice an elongated, but more realistic attack full of slashes, stabs, etc., anywhere on the slow-moving body. The trainer reacts as realistically as possible, which may include actually falling, but still in slow-motion, to allow the trainee to experience the effects of the attack.

**Drill 3:** The trainer attacks with increasing speed, but still reacts as realistically as possible to the trainee's defense. This should get as real as possible.

5

9

6

10

7

11

8

12

# Give and Take

This drill offers skill development just short of complete freestyle knife fighting. Its simplicity is beautiful. You attack. He blocks. He attacks. You block. But the speed and savvy that can be attained doing this is irreplaceable.

Remember to attack on a variety of angles with stabs and slashes.

We start with basic one-step forward and back footwork to create and instruct a pace. Then the "two-attack" drill may train with two steps, three steps and so on. Later, the footwork should and must diminish until the pair is face-to-face fighting like buzz saws.

## Give and take drill 1: One attack drill

a) you step forward and attack on any angle,

b) the partner steps back and executes any block,

c) the partner quickly attacks on any angle,

d) you step back and block,

e) repeat and continue for a set period of time.

## Give and take drill 2: Two attack drill

a) you step forward and attack on any angle with two techniques,

b) the partner steps back and executes two blocks,

c) the partner quickly attacks on any angle with two techniques,

d) you step back and execute two blocks,

e) repeat and continue for a set period of time.

## Give and take drill 3: Three attack drill

Add a third attack.

## Give and take drill 4: Four attack drill

Add a fourth attack.

The next step is freestyle sparring, explained in Chapter 18.

## Double Knife Sinawali

In Filipino Tagalog, Sinawali is loosely translated into "to weave" and when one practices stick or knife Sinawali, one is actually weaving a pattern in the air with their weapons.

Sinawali is primarily associated with "doble bastons" or double sticks, but the patterns can effectively be used to train the knife fighter.

As the rank of Guro, I have collected, practice and teach over 65 different kinds of Filipino Sinawali stick drills, and been exposed to probably twice as many in my training in the United States and the Philippines. But this extensive collection and practice becomes almost an esoteric study of the art, usually not requested, except by the most obsessed Arnisadors.

In a bottom line assessment, just a handful of Sinawali drills offer a prescription to develop many skills for the modern fighter. Timing, coordination, speed, peripheral vision, and strength are just some of the components of the flow, and I can find no other series of exercises in the martial arts quite like Sinawali for enhancing what you've got, or giving you what you haven't yet mastered. That is why I always teach some basic Sinawalis to my street fighting students. And that is why I have included some knife versions in this encyclopedia.

Heaven Sinawali (6 count) is to be performed with two knives. Work this drill as fast as you can. For the purposes of this drill, the starting position is to fold your left arm across your chest so that your left knife hand is near your right armpit area, and hold your right knife hand near your right ear.

**Count 1:** Right hand slashes downward at a 45-degree angle.

**Count 2:** Right hand stops midway and travels to a spot near your left shoulder, as your left hand fires out for a strike.

**Count 3:** Your left hand goes back to your left shoulder and right hand strikes out, then retracts under your left armpit area.

These three steps repeat themselves in opposite action.

**Count 4:** Your left hand slashes downward at a 45-degree angle.

**Count 5:** Left hand stops midway and travels to a spot near your right shoulder, as your right hand fires out for a strike.

**Count 6:** Your right hand goes back to your right shoulder, and your left hand strikes out, then retracts to under or near your armpit area.

1

2

3

4

5

6

7

8

## Variations

a) Once you are "flying," walk around or include footwork.

b) Thrust kick on counts 1 and 4.

c) Work with a partner, hitting blades. Move. Kick.

d) Slightly change some angle deliveries. You might strike low on beats 2 and 5.

e) Work with one hand empty, and use it as a "slapper."

In the Congress knife video "Knife Street Fighter Progression Drills," the Sinawali drill pattern is carried to a multitude of quick kill impact disarms buzz-saw combat scenarios.

# The Throw Away

No knife fighting encyclopedia could be complete without a mention of the true art and skill of throwing the knife. Now I come from the "old school" where the question is always asked, "Why throw away a perfectly good knife!" But I am sure our imaginations can conjure a scenario were there is absolutely nothing else left to do but throw the blade at the opponent. And from a self defense standpoint, this tactic must be reviewed should you possibly be on the receiving end of such a technique.

Whether stabbing or throwing a knife, penetrating the human body in a significant manner, to do substantial damage, is simply not a given. You may strike bone. The opponent may be wearing thick clothing, etc. You need force to penetrate, force that is not controllable after the knife leaves the hand.

Have you ever thrown a knife into a cardboard box for practice only to discover the box had books inside, or some other hard items? The knife pierces the cardboard but stops at the book. The knife then flops down and limply dangles, its tip barely holding on. Think of skin as the cardboard and bone as the book. If you were thrusting the blade in by hand and met opposition, you could increase the force accordingly, or instinctively twist the blade. But once you toss it, that baby is gone! And of course the adage comes into play, that now the bad guy can use the weapon against you.

To overcome this problem, one would have to be a moving target expert, hitting fleshy pathways to sudden death.

Lets explore the factors against throwing the knife successfully:

1) You must be a calm expert to hit a moving target in the right body part. This, in a life and death situation, is far worse than throwing a fastball strike in the ninth inning of the last game of the World Series. Even pros can't guarantee such a high-stress strike.

2) If you are throwing a flipping blade, and the opponent changes the distance between you slightly, it throws the blade flip, rotation calculation, off.

3) The opponent cannot be wearing thick clothing over target body parts.

4) The opponent must be in proper range for the force to succeed. The force diminishes the further the blade flies.

5) You don't need your knife anymore, or for at least the few moments it might take to retrieve it from a partially wounded or dead man. If your target is only wounded, and your knife is dangling tip first in him, he might have been unarmed once, but not now! He has your knife.

6) Most knives are not aerodynamically engineered to be thrown.

7) If you miss, where in the world will your knife wind up? Down a sewer? Half a block away? Inside an innocent bystander or hostage? Or just lost in the environment, depending upon where you are? Or in the hand of the enemy after he picks it up?

I am sure there are knife throwing experts who could hit their man. But it takes practice to master a flipping or a straight-flight blade. I truly believe such masters are rare.

## Knives are commonly thrown three ways

1) from a traditional saber grip for a "football" or "baseball" pitch throw,
2) from a knife tip grip for an end-over-end flipping throw,
3) from an inside-the-palm grip for an underhand type throw.

## Countering the thrown knife

As a knife fighter, you should be able to recognize these throwing grips, if your opponent takes to them in front of you. To counter the airborne knife:

a) Get ready to move! Distance variation will be critical.
b) Get a shield.
c) Bat the blade.

## Throwing the knife

I am no knife throwing expert, but I will advise you to find a blade with little-to-no handle, and blade heavy in an off-balance. Practice up close to a target at first and start throwing from different grips. Master the feel of success and step back. Then repeat this process. Step back and throw. Success. Step back and throw, etc. While this is fun, think about the pitfalls of trying this in the chaos of a real fight.

Then see what it takes to make your favorite knife fly with some success, be it a folder or fixed blade. Good luck, and I truly hope you will never have to throw away your knife in a street fight.

## Chapter 17

# Knife Fighting Combat Scenarios

You may think a knife fight consists of stabs and slashes on the offensive and grabs and passes on the defensive. Could it all be that simple? If that were the case, then a gunfight must be as simple as point and pull the trigger, right? Who needs the police academy, military basic training, Gunsite or Thunder Ranch? If you told a pro football coach that to complete a touchdown you must only catch the ball and run, the coach would call you a simpleton! Why practice? Why make plans? Others think knife training is little more than sword fencing. Many think it is little more than a Filipino drill called Sumbrada where you disarm your enemy like magic each time your knife touches his or her arm. Others just duel like fencers. If this is what you think, you are dead wrong!

There is no doubt that the more deadly the weapon, the easier it is to use effectively. Still all weapons practice, like all physical performance, requires crisis rehearsal in realism. What might really happen and where? Under what light conditions? On what terrain? What will the enemy use as a weapon? Years of police and Army training make me ask these questions. Aside from gun fighting, these combat answers are the most important in the science of knife fighting.

### The Real World

First, martial, criminal and military history tells us many things about real world, empty hand vs. knife, and knife vs. knife combat. Once explored, the chaos and variety is shocking and pushes one to think outside the martial art box when organizing a competent training program. Without this encyclopedia of knowledge, it is easy to ignore or miss whole problem areas.

The following information provides an overview of the combat scenarios of the knife course training modules I structured based on years of research. These provide the varied battlegrounds one needs to train and crisis rehearse. A collection of combat scenarios comes packaged into these training modules. The term module, in this case, means a complete study on that subject.

## The Major SF Congress Knife Counter-Knife Combat Training Modules are:

1) Command and Mastery of Edged Weapons (solo development)
2) Quick Draws and Counters to Quick Draws
3) Killshot! Knife Fencing and Dueling
4) Sinawali Street Fighter (when the impact disarm works)
5) Chain of the Knife (when the impact disarm doesn't work)
6 Alley Cat Street Fighter (extreme close quarter combat, anti-crime material)
7) Ground Zero: Knife Ground Fighting
8) Use of Force - The Capture and Contain Module (many less-than-lethal tactics)
9) Do or Die - Unarmed vs. the Knife
10) The British Bastard Mix (knife fighting vs. other weapons)
11) The Archipelago Module (martial skill drills from the islands of the Pacific)
12) Special Operations Module (for military only)

Each module or package-approach includes:
1) education and execution of the fundamentals
2) flow drill practice to support skill development
3) how to trouble shoot and problem solve the movements
4) how to counter the movements
5) how to right-handed, left-handed and righty vs. lefty problem solve
6) how to crisis rehearse, that is learn to fight in complete, realistic combat scenarios
7) how to seamlessly integrate all weapons and ranges of standing, kneeling and prone combat

This chapter covers crisis rehearsal of steps taken in combat, all building combat simulations - the combat scenario. Remember my lifesaving mantra? The bigger the knife - the less kick boxing and jujitsu like skills you need. The smaller the knife - the more you need. The knife serves as a great equalizer, but it is not God's gift to equalization. The following pages demonstrate combat scenarios from just a few of the modules listed above. You may find more information about these combat scenarios in the other chapters of this volume and in *Volume 2: Military Knife Combat.*

## Quick Draw: The Knife Acquisition Module

This module teaches the folder and fixed blade, primary, secondary and tertiary carry sites. The student learns to draw from these sites, open the blade quickly and, if necessary, quietly. We emphasize and assess grips, strategies and tactics. Once the quick draws are identified and practiced, this module instructs the counters to these quick draws as expressed through early-phase, mid-phase and late-phase tactics. The overall performance is eventually expressed through combat scenarios. Here is but one scenario.

## Quick draw combat scenario: Military quick draw and throw

This body throw, a classic among military trainers, is slowly slipping away from most modern study, primarily because the fall is very hard and few charge the trainee with sufficient real world ferocity to make the technique real enough to justify practice. Retired African Combat Vet Captain Ben Mangels showed me this tactic. He was the first to convince me how powerful and necessary this tactic is and how important it is to cover the pommel strike in knife training. In this series I attack Tom Barnhart with a realistic mad rush attack. He pulls his knife but does not have the split second necessary to bring the blade into play, so he smashes me with pommel in a key target. The face or, in this case the throat, provides an excellent target. This shot will slow an enemy, but will not stop the dashing madman momentum. With a blade to my throat and a solid grip on me, Tom collapses under the pressure of the run, puts one foot or even two into my pelvis and springs me over. He must get up after the toss and follow-up.

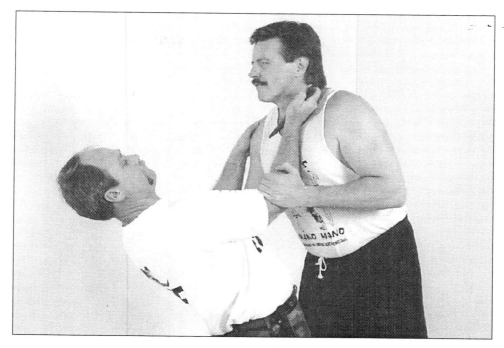

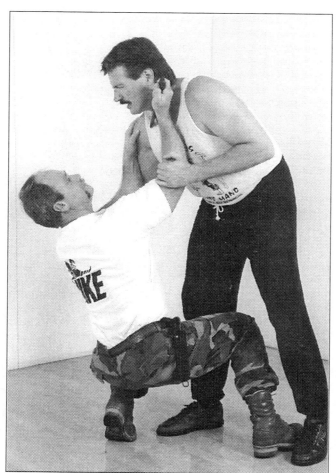

Practice scenarios where you intercept cross draws and other common carry site quick draws. Here I charge in on Barnhart for a Catch and Combat Drill.

## The Spartan Street Fighter Module

Training documented by historians as far back as the Egyptians and Spartans served as a basis for this module. One close quarter combat sword tactic consists of hacking the enemy's arm that holds the sword. In this module you learn to execute the impact upon the weapon-bearing limb and, if the disarm is achieved, to barrage into the opponent in a coordinated, total, full body assault. Learn the four common angles of criminal knife assault and attack, plus the advanced angles that a trained attacker will try.

This package teaches the seamless application of the impact disarm with support hand and leg strikes, trapping hands, then using the knife as a takedown/grappling tool. The bigger the knife, such as a kukri, bolo of big Bowie, then the less kickboxing-like and jujitsu-like skills you will need to fight on. The smaller your knife, like the size of a tactical folder, the more physical fighting skills you need to survive. Performance is ultimately expressed though combat scenarios. If the impact disarm does not work, its brother module The Chain of the Knife comes next.

For combat scenario practice, have your trainer attack you with the 12 angles of attack. Then you use some evasive footwork as you blast the weapon-bearing limb with your knife. In this module, the impact disarm works. Each time your trainer drops the knife, and you explode in taking every available knife attack, strike and kick you can until the enemy presumably goes down and out. In this format you have 12 action-packed combat scenarios.

## Chain of the Knife Module

This module comes into play when the above Spartan impact strike upon the weapon-bearing limb fails to cause a disarm! This can happen! You are in close, and he is still armed! Possibly diminished, but still deadly! Still armed and dangerous. You must try first to seize the hand/forearm and fight on from there. This seizure is the first link in the chain of survival-thus its nickname. You must learn passing skills and footwork evasion skills here in case your initial catch fails and the weapon is still coming in. This module includes troubleshooting the enemy's free hand, quick kill targets, trapping hands, using the knife as a grappling tool, and performance is ultimately expressed through combat scenarios. Many commando tactics are revealed in this very combative module. The Win Mentality, taught in special police and military courses, is emphasized. Here are two of some 20 combat scenarios.

## Chain of the knife combat scenario 1:

Here Hock hits the weapon-bearing limb,

but the enemy retains his knife. Hock must grab and hang on for dear life! He tries a knife attack, but the enemy grabs that. With the simple use of his elbow to lift and smash downward to release the grip, the attack continues. Finish, as always, with a takedown.

1

2

3

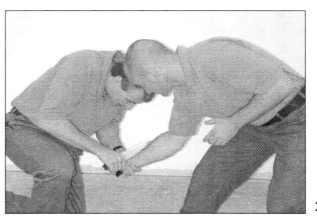

4

1

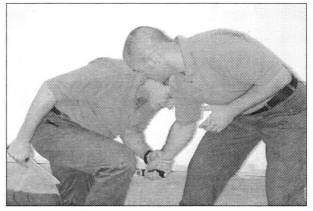

5

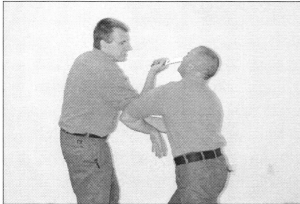

2

## Chain of the knife combat scenario 2: The commando crotch kill

Here we emphasize the win mentality. The enemy stabs you, and the force of the attack drops you to your knee. Your link to survival is to hold the weapon-bearing limb. You deliver the powerful stab to the under side of the crotch, a violent, shocking stab. Twist the blade to open the wound canal and use it in the crook of the arm to pull the enemy down. A shin to the weapon-bearing limb captures the knife arm, and you finish the enemy. As you may well fall and die yourself from your wound, take the son of a bitch with you.

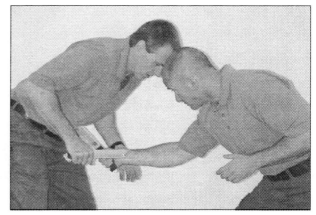

3

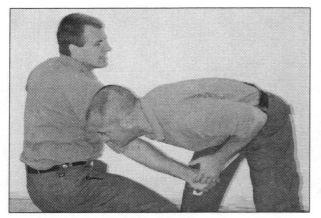

4

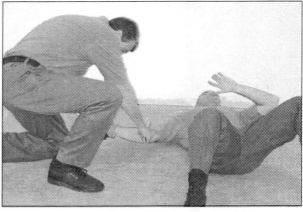

7

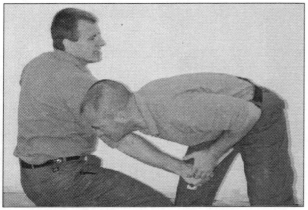

5

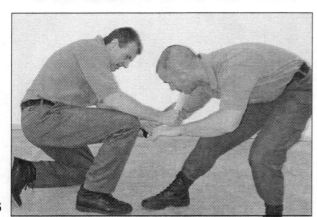

6

## In the clutches of:

This extreme close quarter combat training module covers situations when the enemy has his hand on your weapon-bearing limb and you have your hand on his. Here we practice flow drills, kicking drills, kicking drills, problem solving and counters. This close quarter combat predicament may happen as often, or more often than dueling. These clutches may occur knee high and prone. Scientifically, this breaks into four clutching possibilities to develop skills from:

*High in the clutches of:*

*Low in the clutches of:*

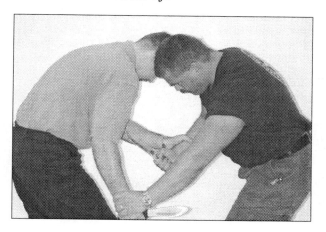

*Mixed in the clutches of:*
*a) high and low*
*b) righty vs. lefty*

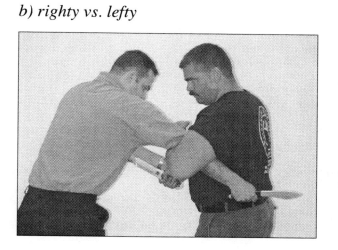

*Arm wrap traps:*

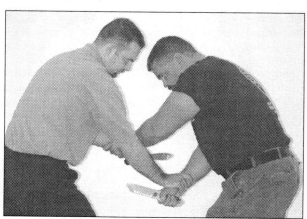

## High catch in the clutches of combat scenario 1:

1

2

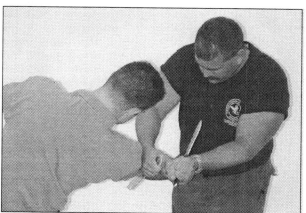

3

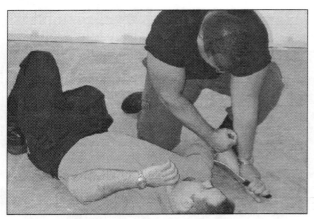

4

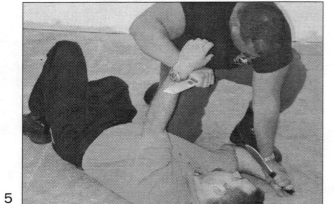

5

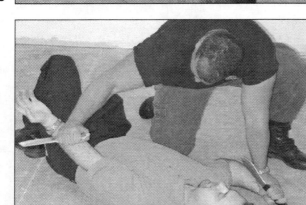

6

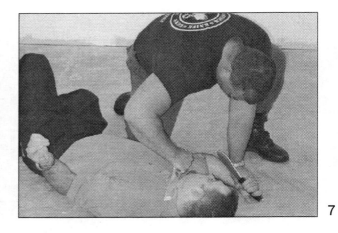

7

## Low catch in the clutches of combat scenario 2:

The after stab follow-ups may vary. Here we demonstrate a Filipino based takedown.

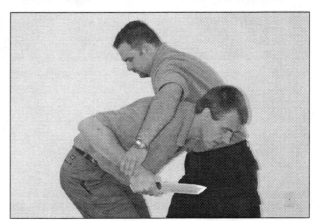

1

2

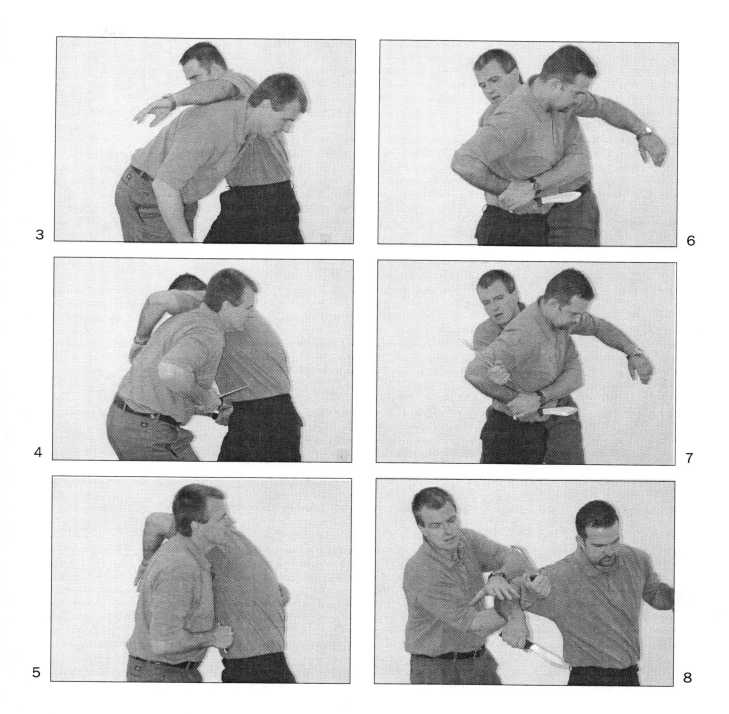

3

6

4

7

5

8

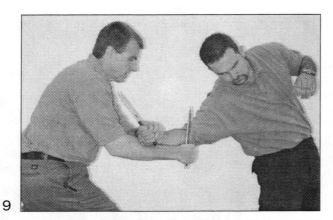

9

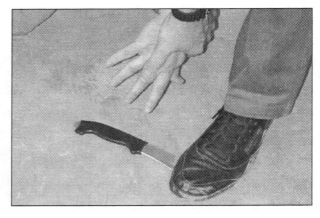

13

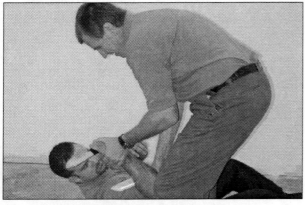

10

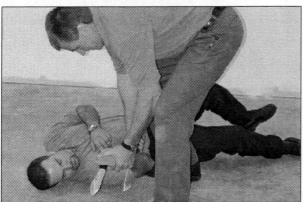

11

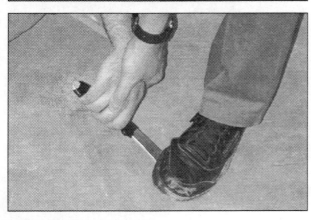

12

## Alley Cat: Anti-Street Crime Module

This extreme close quarter combat module develops your use of a reverse grip in common street attacks, muggings and robberies, either from the concealed and ready grip, or drawn into action to a reverse grip from a quick draw. Learn common deceptions, tricks and street attacks of criminals-such as the Wild Pack Attack. This package develops with flow drills, trapping hands, targeting skills and using the knife as a grappling tool. Performance is expressed through combat scenarios. Here are two of these scenarios.

## End of the choker scenario 1:

In this series a cocky criminal approaches and holds your throat. Unbeknownst to him, you detect his approach and place your knife in a concealed grip down by your side. A frightened expression or words of compliance may give him a false sense of security. You slash up on and grab upon his weapon-bearing limb, push away the hand and attack the throat of this still-armed and deadly dangerous felon. You hammer down on the crook of his arm for a takedown.

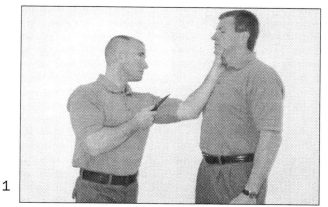

1

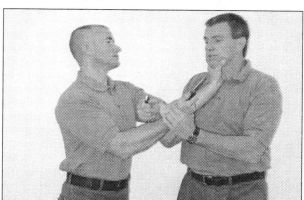

2

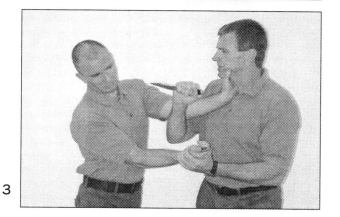

3

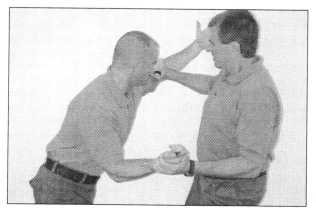

4

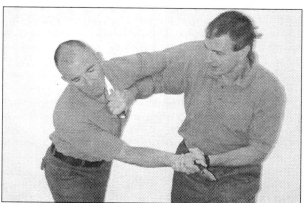

5

6

## End of the choker scenario 2:

You free your neck of the grip, pull your tactical folder and further free your neck of danger by striking the arm of the attacker. You may use the folder as palm stick unopened, or open it for lethal damage.

Remember this scenario may fit when multiple dangerous attackers surround you. Taking out one with your blade, in order to face the others may serve as a legal self-defense option! Practice both.

4

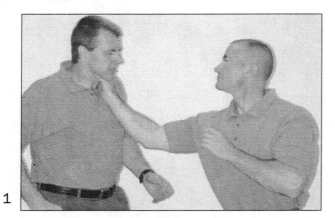

1

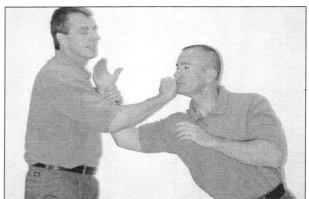

5

2

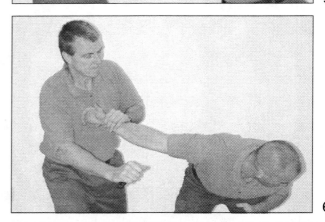

6

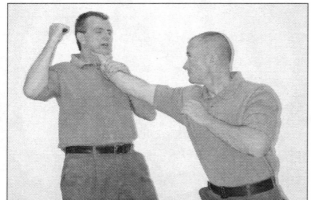

3

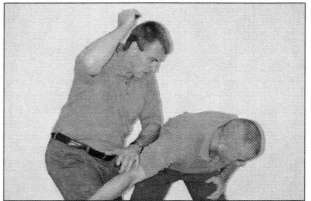

7

8

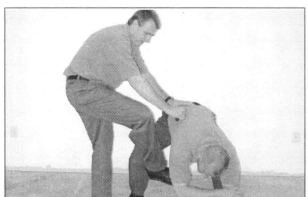

9

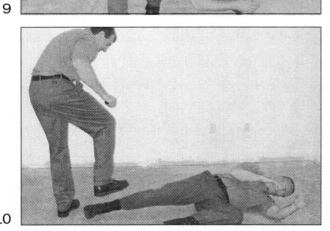

10

## Ground Zero: The Knife Ground Fighting Module

This is a module on knife ground fighting from knee high, side-by-side, top-side and bottom-side predicaments to include quick draws under horizontal stress, and the use of saber or reverse grips in extremely close-quarters. It includes all types of dirty tricks like groin rips and biting. Performance is expressed through combat scenarios. Real-world predicaments and common submission ground fighting tactics are dissected. *This is the most overlooked area in knife training, yet many civilians, soldiers and police sustain injuries or die on Ground Zero.*

## Kick the face series:

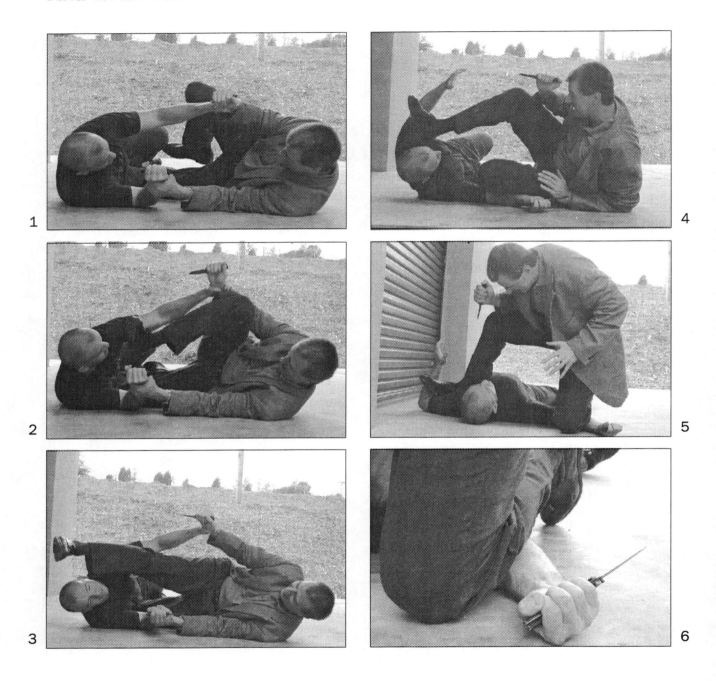

1

2

3

4

5

6

## The Paladin dismount:

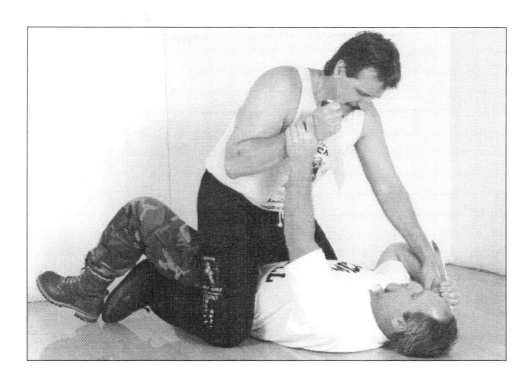

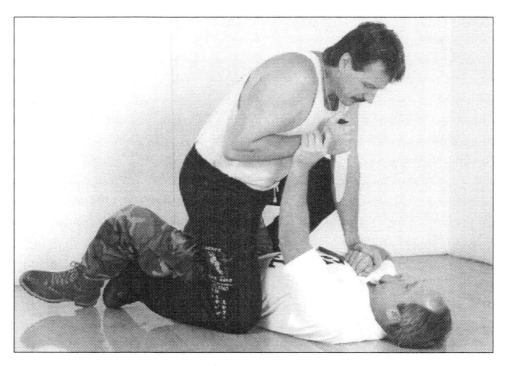

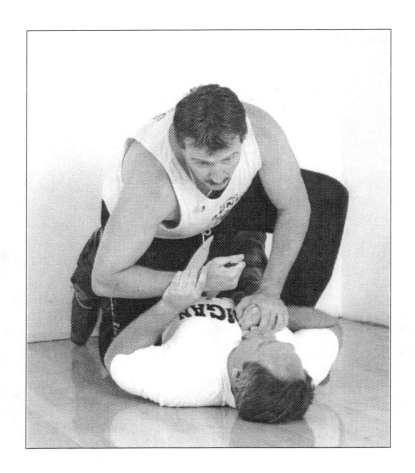

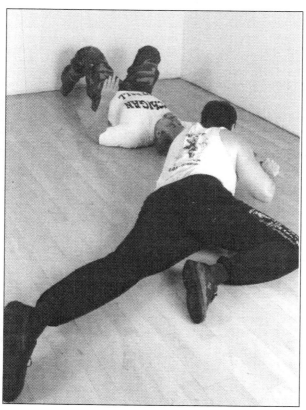

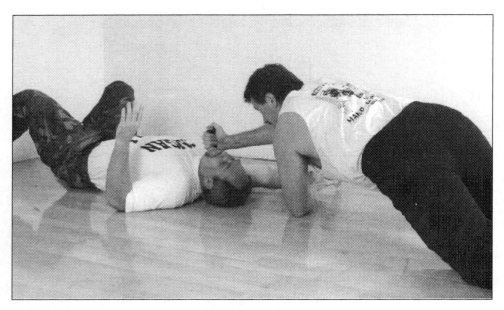

Here Hock shows the Paladin dismount to a group of US Marines attending their Close Quarter Battle Instructor's course in Quantico.

Volume 2 and an entire section in this encyclopedia feature additional scenarios totally dedicated to Ground Zero Knife Fighting.

## Do or Die: The Unarmed vs. the Knife Module

This module covers strategies and tactics on how to face the armed attacker when you are unarmed and cannot or should not escape. Use of the environment, evasion footwork, and The Diminished Fighter Theory are emphasized, along with the desperate topics of Do or Die knife disarming. In addition, we cover the popular Military vs. the Knife Combat Drill (highlighted here). The module organizes and prioritizes grabbing and passing skills. It develops hand/arm and leg attack drills along with takedowns, throws and ground finishes, all ultimately expressed through combat scenarios. Here we cover two VERY basic presentations.

## The catch progression scenario 1:

Any catch, any kick, any strike, any takedown is basic formula. There are many variations to work on.

2

3

1

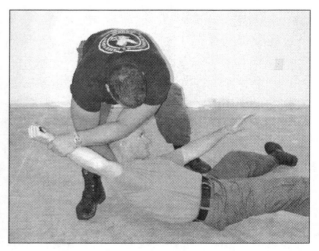

4

## The pass progression scenario 2:

Miss the catch? Any pass, any strike, then any catch, any strike, any takedown. Again there are many training variations.

## The British Bastard Mix Module

Inspired by British SAS (which inspired many military and police units) and commando training, this module covers our knife vs. other common weapons like baseball bats, shovels, sticks, canes - even some anti-gun - threat uses. Various combat scenarios quantify skills. Here we demonstrate two of the many combat scenarios.

## Scenario 1: The impact weapon attack

Here, a subject attacks with an impact weapon, in this case a baseball bat. Evasive footwork helps us dodge the first blast. Hopefully the miss will cause the enraged attacker to over swing, allowing for setup time. In the early phase of the next attack, Hock cuts, throw the arms, wheels the opponent down and follows up.

1

2

3

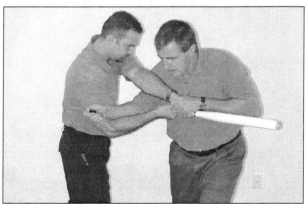

4

5

6

2

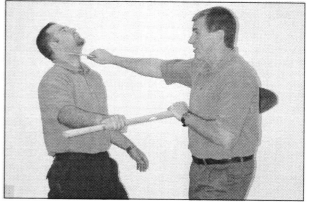

7

3

## Scenario 2: The shovel attack

Many military units pack a shovel in their kit or gear, for a variety of reasons, from digging a foxhole to get below surface enemy gunfire, filing sandbags to swinging it in last ditch combat. Some armies, like Russian Spetsnaz carry shovels like edged weapons and practice throwing them like axes.

4

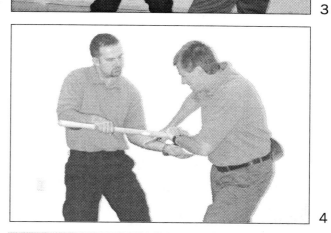

5

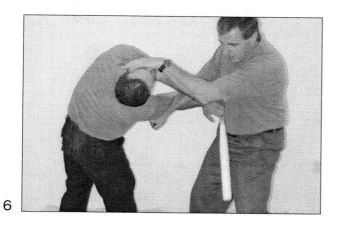

1

6

7

8

9

10

# The S.O.M. - The Special Operations Module

Taught ONLY to the official militaries of our country and its allies, this training involves surprise battlefield assault, urban and rural sentry killing, plus pursuit and kill, dirty tricks and related operational material. S.O.M. was nicknamed once by a Marine Sergeant who attended my course as the murder course - hence the public restriction. I will show only one of these extremely aggressive and violent scenarios, meant only to kill the enemies of our country, as well as to prepare our allies against such surprise attacks.

1

## The end of the walking guard

At the point of an infiltrated attack, when silence is broken, or when a troop walks away from the earshot of his comrades, the soldier hides behind cover, as simulated in the first photo below. The soldier attacks behind the knee in beat with the enemy guard's step. The soldier circles the blade into the pelvis-both a deadly stabbing target and a torso balance breakaway point - and with a handhold pulls the enemy down for a finish.

2

3

(You may find more on the subject of military tactics in *Volume 2: Military Knife Combat*)

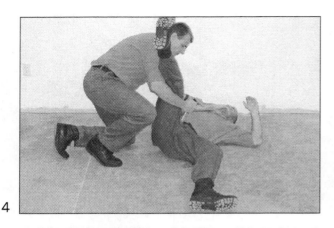

4

6

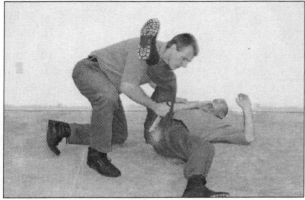

5

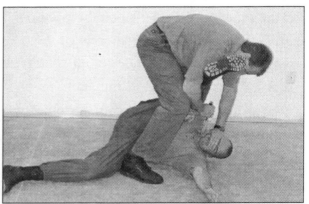

7

## In the Final Analysis

Knife fighting is not just about the slash, stab, pass and grab. It is not just about sparring and Filipino Sumbrada. Nor is it just a lot of flow drills. Drills build the scenarios. Recognize the history of the urban and rural battlefields and crisis-rehearse these situations.

Hock teaching U. S. Marine advanced combat instructors some knife ground fighting strategies at Quantico, Virginia in 1999.

# RANK TRAINING

## OVERALL RANK LEVELS

Hock is a recognized 10th Dan Grandmaster/Founder by one of the largest martial arts Grandmaster groups in the world – The World Global Alliance, as well as other national and international organizations. All rank achieved through the Scientific Fighting Congress is respected and recognized. If you are interested in rank and instructorships, each course exists in a separate progression some material overlaps and cross training is an option. You may work in one area or all areas.

**Hand to Hand** – Level 1-10
**Archipelago Combat** – Level 1-10
**Knife Counter-Knife** – Level 1-10
**Dos Manos System** – Level 1, 2, 3 (plus instructorships)
*(Additional Dan Black Belt and Master Levels available)*
*(Theme videos that focus on individual skills available in the Knife Counter-Knife System).*

American Combat Kempo (ACK). Hock also empowers you with an American Combat Kempo rank. ACK is a secondary, "support" rank and alternative option/title to the Hand-to-Hand Combat program. The material is the same, but you may choose to teach it in the framework of a Karate-type class, to enhance your business success. Convert appropriate material into a lucrative kid's class. An ACK rank comes free with each H-to-H rank.

### SFC Instructor Levels
1) Class Organizer - leads official workout groups to develop skill
2) Basic Instructor
3) Advanced Instructor
4) Black Belt Degree Instructors

Basic and advanced instructors are not Black Belts but may teach and promote their students up to one rank under their rank. Black Belts may become instructors upon request. A one-time $50 fee for Basic; and $50 for Advanced Instructorships. Basic Instructorships start at Level 5.

### Must Instructors Teach only Congress Material?
NO! You are free to do as you wish. Some Congress instructors...
1) Exclusively teach Congress material.
2) Run Congress courses in their school or other schools.
3) Mix Congress material into their existing program.
4) Lease time in schools, gyms, rec centers, etc.
5) Use their backyards and garages.
6) Travel and develop their own seminar circuit.
7) Are instructors involved in other famous courses.

## HOW DO I TRAIN?

The SF Congress has members in 26 different countries that train and/or network thru *Close Quarter Combat Magazine*, with over 75 instructors and even more class organizers with whom you may train. Hock travels to more than 30 states and overseas several times each year. Train...
1) With Congress area instructors and organizers.
2) With Hock in seminars, camps, privates and semi-privates.
3) To acquire the rank and theme videos, the books and manuals.
4) And test for the first 3 levels by home/video testing.

Hock offers two full day private training sessions in your area before or after the seminars. This includes any rank and instructorship fees you achieve. You need a workout partner. Weekdays are best!
1) $1,200 for one person (you need a "stuntman" to work with)
2) $850 for two more interested people (per person)
3) $2,500 for a group of 10 or more (plus expenses)

Host a seminar? There are several programs available. Base your plan on a minimum of 25 or more people and it can happen anywhere! Call Hock for details.

## HOW DO I GET STARTED?

It's simple. Just order the first level of any of the four courses.
- Hand to Hand
- Knife/Counter Knife
- Archipelago Combatives
- Dos Manos System (DMS)

or start with The Foundation – *The Knife Fighting Encyclopedia*

## The CLOSE QUARTER COMBATIVE GROUP

You may progress in separate programs or cross-train in all. Remember, courses are based upon the essence of combat, and some material overlaps. If you rank in all three courses, you begin to amass certification in the CQC-Group, an elite insider group with special expertise in the Congress.

## JOIN THE SFC THROUGH MEMBERSHIP PROGRAMS.

**Program 1**: U.S. residents $30. Canadian residents $50. Outside the U.S. and Canada residents $70. This one-year membership connects you with a special group of police officers, military, martial artists and aware civilians, and entitles you to the bi-monthly publication *Close Quarter Combat Magazine*. (Certificates available upon request)

**Program 2:** Visit the webpage at www.HocksCQC.com or ask about special video purchase packages that include membership and magazine.

# S.F. CONGRESS VIDEO, BOOK & CLOTHING SUPPLY CATALOG

## HAND TO HAND COMBAT
____ Hand to Hand Combat Level 1
____ Hand to Hand Combat Level 2
____ Hand to Hand Combat Level 3
____ Hand to Hand Combat Level 4
____ Hand to Hand Combat Level 5
____ Hand to Hand Combat Level 6
____ Hand to Hand Combat Level 7
____ Hand to Hand Combat Level 9
____ Hand to Hand Combat Level 10: The Black Belt Test
____ Ground Zero! Ground Kick Fighting
*Level 8 under production*

## FILIPINO COMBATIVES VIDEOS
____ Level 1: Yellow Belt
____ Level 2: Blue Belt
____ Level 3: Blue One Stripe
____ Level 4: Green Belt
____ Level 5: Green One Stripe
____ Level 6: Green Two Stripes
____ Level 7: Brown Belt
____ Doble Baston – The Filipino Double Sticks
*Levels 8, 9, 10 under production*

## KNIFE COMBATIVES VIDEOS
____ Level 1,2,3: Journeyman Series (2 hrs) $49.95
____ Level 4: Tradesman Series
____ Level 5: Tradesman Series
____ Level 6: Expert 3rd Class
*Levels 7, 8, 9, 10 under production*

## KNIFE THEME VIDEOS
____ Knife Showdown! Dueling / Fencing / Sparring
____ Knife Trapping Hands
____ Knife "Combat the Mad Rush Attack"
____ Knife "Combat the Torso Stab Attack"
____ "Sinawali" and "Alleycat" Knife Fighter Systems
____ Chain of the Knife System
____ "Do or Die!" Unarmed vs. the Knife
____ Tactical Folder for Handgun Retention (New!)
____ Knife Command and Mastery: Solo Practice Methods (New!)
____ In the Clutches of (New!)

## DMS: CLOSE QUARTER STICK GRAPPLING/FIGHTING
____ DMS 1: DMS Strikes, Blocks and Drills
____ DMS 2: DMS Combat Scenarios
____ DMS 3: DMS Ground Fighting, the Push, Pull and Turn Series

## TRAINING MANUALS
(Purchase only if you work actively in the system or have videos to which you may refer.)
____ The Hand-to-Hand Combat Course $25 plus $6 postage
____ The Filipino Combatives Course $25 plus $6 postage
____ The Knife Combatives Course $25 plus $6 postage

## BOOKS (bookstore quality, oversized paperbacks)
____ *The Knife Fighting Encyclopedia Vol. 1: The Foundation.* 318 pages, 1,000 how-to photos $35 plus $6 postage
____ *The Knife Fighting Encyclopedia Vol. 2: Military Knife Combat.* 205 pages, 187 how-to photos $25 plus $6 postage

## T-SHIRTS
____ Congress Logo T-Shirts. Shirts are dark blue with gold Congress logo, small on front and large logo on back. $25 plus $2.50 postage

____ Congress Logo Sleeveless T-Shirts. Shirts are black bearing upper arms. Not a tank top. Small logo on front, big on back. $25 plus 2.50 postage

____ Close Quarter Combatives T-Shirts. Shirts are military OD with Close Quarter Combat inscription across the chest in stencil and Congress logo on front and back. $25 plus $2.50 postage (most popular!)

## CLOSE QUARTER COMBAT MAGAZINE
(Back issues are $10, $2 postage. One year subscription $30)
____ CQCMAG Back Issues #1, #2, #3, #4 (circle one)

## TRAINING KNIVES
____ Official Congress Metal Training Knife "The Big Belly" Fixed Blade with Congress logo on blade. $39.95 plus $5 postage
____ Official Congress Metal Training Knife "The Normal" Fixed Blade with Congress logo on blade. $39.95 plus $5 postage
____ Official Congress Metal Training Knife "The Combat Folder Simulator," Congress logo on blade. $39.95 plus $5 postage

## ORDER SPECS
* Each video is $30 with $6 postage and handling except JMan 1, 2, 3, (2 hrs) which sells for $49.95

* Add an additional $25 postage International orders (not including Canada).

* CQCMagazine and SFC membership $30

* Canadian subscription/membership $50

* Overseas subscription/membership $70 (Membership certificates available upon request)

* We accept MC/Visa/Discover/AmExpress, money order or personal checks.

* Payable to: Lauric Enterprises, Inc., P.O. Box 5372, Fort Oglethorpe, GA 30742, or call (706) 866-2656 or fax order to (706) 866-2657

NAME: _____

ADDRESS: _____

CITY: _____

STATE: _____ ZIP: _____ PHONE: _____

CREDIT CARD TYPE: _____

CARD NO.: _____

EXP: _____

Subtotal _____

Plus Postage _____

Total: _____